JEFF LEAKE

TWELVE TRENDS
IN MULTIPLICATION

A Study in Reproducing Churches

ISBN 978-1-09837-296-5 eBook 978-1-09837-297-2

CONTENTS

FORWARD

My whole family came to Christ at a church plant. Crossroads Community Church started at Columbia High School, and this was before it was common for churches to meet in public schools. I remember being there the first day and having to help grab additional chairs off the metal rolling chair rack as more and more people kept showing up. It was incredibly exciting seeing so many people interested in gathering to hear about Jesus.

My Sunday-school teacher, Mr. Bell was a one-eyed National Collegiate wrestling champion. As a seven-year-old, I gave him my undivided attention. Our class met under the football stadium bleachers. It was in that classroom where I asked Jesus to be Lord of my life. Little did I know that four decades later I would be serving as the Director of Church Multiplication Network, working to resource and relationally connect other people who had a dream to start a church. This church, like others you're about to read about, represents the many trends in church planting across the nation.

Every week I get a front row seat to witness the beauty and diversity of The Church. Whether they're making disciples in a rural, urban, suburban or anything in-between setting, the gospel of Jesus is being propelled. Jesus said he'd build his church and Jeff Leake has taken him at his word. Jeff is a mentor and multiplier who serves on the CMN Lead Team. He is also a champion for church planters, a practitioner himself, modeling a multiplication mindset, having assisted in 31 church plants and counting.

The Church Multiplication Network exists to see a healthy church in every community that's marked by spiritual and numerical growth. Every church that is planted shares similarities and uniqueness based on their context, approach, and leadership. This book is a reminder that there's not a *way* to plant a church but rather multiple *ways*.

The church exists to reach people who have not yet experienced God's grace. We're all invited to join Jesus on his mission to seek and to save the lost. The following multiplication stories give us a look at 12 trends in church multiplication. I'm so grateful that Jeff captured these stories and transferred them into a format with which we can engage. May this book stir our faith, remind us of Jesus' love for the lost, and lead us further into church multiplication.

In your corner cheering loudly,
Dr. Jeffery Portmann
Director of Church Multiplication Network U.S.A.

INTRODUCTION

One of the greatest joys of my life has been the joy of multiplication! I absolutely love starting something new, believing in someone's dream, reaching a new community, and hearing the stories of changed lives that result from that effort. There is nothing quite like it.

It is early in 2021, as I write this, and this year marks the 25th anniversary since we helped to plant our very first church. It was in the spring of 1996. I had been the lead pastor of Allison Park Church for five years. We were growing, but we were land-locked and had no apparent space to expand with our current facility.

Honestly, church planting was not on my mind at all. I was just trying to survive as a young pastor and wanting to find solutions for my church to continue to grow. Allison Park Church is located in the north suburbs of Pittsburgh, Pennsylvania. It has been in existence since 1966. I had worked for the founding pastor, as an associate, and was now serving as his successor after he departed to become the pastor of a church in California.

While I was praying one afternoon, I felt God's prompting to start planting churches. My request to God was that he would open up property for us and help us raise the money to build a bigger building! For whatever reason, we had hit a wall and could not seem to find a solution that was right for us. I was frustrated. I was venting my frustrations in prayer.

Then God spoke to me.

"I can hear that you have a problem," is what I sensed that the Holy Spirit was whispering to me. To which I responded aloud, "Yes, God! We do have a problem, and it seems that you are not offering any solutions here!" Then I heard, "Have you considered that I have problems too?" This left me speechless for a moment. Then I said, "What problems? You are God! You have it all. You can do it all."

"My problem is your city. Your region is filled with towns and communities that need a life-giving church. My solution to your problem is that you would put my problem first. I need you to put the reaching of your city ahead of the growth of your church."

I'm not sure if you have ever had a moment like this? God was impressing on my spirit some very clear thoughts that were obviously not in line with what I even wanted to hear! But I recognized that same warm impression that I have come to know as the presence of God in my life. When I sensed that prompting, I felt a strong conviction that this was a leading from God.

So I said, 'Yes! I will put your problem first, Lord. We will seek to plant churches and not so much worry about our own growth." This immediately reminded me of the promise Jesus said in Matthew 6:33: "Seek first the kingdom of God and his righteousness, and all these things will be added unto you as well."[1] Based on that word, we stepped out in faith.

At that time, in the church world, there were not models to follow as to how to do this. There was no Church Multiplication Network from which to consult or get training and resources. I was a young man (32 years old) with zero experience in planting churches. But we were naive enough and obedient enough to try.

We set a goal to plant one church each year, in our region, for the next five years. We started with Crossway Church in Mars, PA, located about 12 miles north of Allison Park Church. The church opened in November of 1996 and continues to be a great church to this day. Somehow, we completed that plan to plant our first five churches.

Then God opened up property for us to build a new building for APC and expand our ministry as well. It was Matthew 6:33 being fulfilled before our very eyes. Since that time, sending our spiritual sons and daughters to plant new churches has continued to be a part of our vision and DNA. We have now multiplied directly by sending out 31 church planters over the years.

Many of our 'daughter churches' have also reproduced (and even some granddaughter churches) so that a movement of more than 100 new churches has been birthed during the last 25 years.

During that same timeframe, church multiplication has become a science of sorts. There are many organizations out there like Church Multiplication Network, New Thing Network, Stadia, Exponential, Association of Related Churches (ARC), Acts 29 Network, and more that have been established to help train and resource church planters.

I have personally served on the Lead Team of the Church Multiplication Network since its inception in 2007 and have had a front row seat to the waves of new churches that have been planted. But the multiplication trends go beyond church planting. During this same season, we have seen a brand new way of doing church begin.

It's the multi-site movement, now with more than 8,000 churches across America who function with more than one location.

I will never forget attending one of the first multi-site conferences in 2003, at North Coast in San Diego, California. It was there I heard the stories of Seacoast Church (Pastor Greg Surratt), New Community Church (Pastor Dave Ferguson), and North Coast Church (Larry Osborne) describe this new approach to multi-campus, multi-venue ministry.

All of these innovative entrepreneurial leaders who were pursuing church multiplication were intoxicating for me. I absolutely loved it. I have become a student of sorts, of every kind of creative idea when it comes to multiplication.

For me, it has never been a matter of either/or when it comes to reaching new territories through multiplication. I am absolutely in favor of all innovations that attempt to expand the kingdom. And I love to learn from other leaders!

This passion of mine has led me to do a number of things that I hope will be helpful in this book. First, Allison Park Church has experimented with a lot of different creative concepts in multiplication. We launched a church planting network in 2006. We became a multi-campus church in 2012. For the first few years, we were solely a video venue. Now we are a combination of live teaching and some video teaching in our six physical locations.

We have also tried some different venue services, within our broadcast building (what we now call our Hampton Campus) like an acoustic service, tailored more to suit our older attendees

Some things have worked really well. Other ideas for us fell flat. But in every step we have taken, we have continued to learn and collect ideas about new and creative ways to reach people for Christ.

What I have attempted to do in this book is document some of the trends that are evident in churches that are multiplying. As you will see, each of these models is very unique. But each one carries with it something very powerful and precious. I hope, like me, you will be inspired by the stories that you read.

Here's what I have done for you in this study:

1. **Interviews** - I have done my best to collect the thoughts of some pastors who lead great churches. Many of these

pastors are my close friends. All were very open and willing to share their journey.

2. **Model Descriptions** - In each chapter, I have attempted to draw some distinctions for you about how and why the model works, what it costs, and how you might consider taking some first steps in that particular direction of multiplication.

3. **Contrasts** - Early on, you will start to pick up on some of the differences in values, strategies, and style. This is not to lift one up over the other, but simply to educate you on what is possible.

Too often, our creativity is limited because we see the world in nice neat categories. For instance, most people think of the Attractional/Video Venue Model when they hear the word multisite. But the way to do multi-site ministry is much broader in scope than what anyone realizes.

In fact, I have outlined for you the 12 trends that are the most obvious to me. There might be creative ideas being pursued right now that I have not yet heard about. If you know of some innovation that I have not provided here, please email me at jeffl@ allisonparkchurch.com.

My hope in this book was not to be comprehensive in my description of these trends. My desire was to be practically inspiring. What does that mean? Many of you may have already felt prompted toward church multiplication. My hope is that these stories will inspire you even more, and give God the opportunity to speak to you.

But I also want this material to be practical enough that you can determine the 'how.' Based on the models described, you will have enough information to know which two or three potential paths forward there are for you and your church to prayerfully pursue.

Out of this practical inspiration, I pray that God would create a wave of thousands more churches, campuses, and venues in the future.

May God bless you with an anointing to multiply.
Jeff

PS - Thanks to all the pastors and leaders who were willing to so freely share their stories, their pain, and their philosophies of ministry with us. We are indebted to you for it. **NOTE: all the interviews conducted with the following pastors were held at the beginning of the 2020 pandemic. Therefore, all stories and stats reflect pre-pandemic realities.**

MODEL #1:
THE ATTRACTIONAL/VIDEO VENUE

At the first meeting of River Valley Church, 13 peo-ple showed up. Only four of them were not related to the pastor, Rob Ketterling, or weren't promised a job at the church when the church could afford them. Of those four, two never came back. It was not exactly the most auspicious start to a church. Ketterling wrote about what it was like for them in the beginning:

This was in 1995, and we started River Valley Church in a school, but I immediately began looking for a permanent home for us. As it always happens, with new church startups, the people who attended often asked, 'Pastor Rob, when are we getting our own building?' I told them again and again, mostly believing in faith, "I don't know, but I'm sure God has something wonderful for us."

I eventually found an empty field on the corner of a key intersection in Apple Valley, Minnesota, where four communities converge. It was close and appeared to be a prime location for the future. I often walked through the field, and prayed, "Lord, someday I'd love for You to let us build a church on this corner."[2]

About four years into the life of River Valley Church, God began to do a miracle through a series of divine appointments and risk-taking steps of faith that led to the eventual construction of the church's first official building and grand opening in September, 2000. Prior to moving into this new building, the church had an average attendance of 270 people.

Soon after making the move, the church began to rapidly grow. "I was beginning to ask God, 'What do you want us to do now? **Are we going to build a bigger building so that we can be a bigger church in this location? Or do you want us to go multi-site?'** Ketterling said. "And as I continued to present this question to God in prayer, I felt God say to me, 'You are going to be a multi-site church, and as a confirming sign of this, someone is going to give you a building!'"

It was not long after God gave Rob that specific promise, that the District Superintendent of the Minnesota District, Clarence St John, called Ketterling and said "There is a church in Faribault that is potentially donating its building. Are you interested?" In Ketterling's office, at that moment, was a map that the leaders used for prayer. On that map, there were several post-it notes, stuck on various communities and cities that would be potential locations for multiplication. One of those post-it notes was hanging on the map, with the name FARIBAULT written boldly upon it.

"For me, this was like the Macedonian vision that God had given Paul. It was as if someone was appearing to say, 'Come over to Faribault and help us,'" Ketterling said. But this was more than just a confirming request, it came with a confirming sign. This church had a building that was worth one million dollars. There were only 40 people left, and they were facing the hard reality that they needed to do something different if they were going to stay alive.

At first, some of the members were reluctant to just hand over the keys. In his book, *Fix It*, Ketterling recounted the reaction to that moment and what happened next:

"I gave my presentation to the group and invited questions. It was obvious that a faction sitting near the back was hostile to me and our church. They had their arms crossed, and the look on their faces screamed, 'Over my dead body!' There was, I was sure, sadness mixed with anger. They had devoted their lives to the church, and it had come to this moment when they needed to keep the doors open.

"On our tour the previous afternoon, the deacons had been positive, and the people who sat near them seemed equally optimistic that this arrangement could work well for everybody. The current pastor and his wife were there, but they weren't really engaged. They were planning to leave the church as soon as the deal—any deal—was done.

"Some of the questions about the multi-site model were straightforward, the kind you'd expect anyone to ask. Then one of the men in the back stood up and growled, 'Our building is worth a million dollars. I want to know what your motive is for being here.' At that moment, I sensed the Holy Spirit say, 'Tell them now.'

"I took a deep breath and announced to him, and everyone else in the room. 'On my driver's license, it says that if I die, I am an organ donor.' I had no idea what to say after that sentence, but the Holy Spirit downloaded what came next. 'When

I die, I want the doctors to take everything useful in me and give it to the living who need it. I don't want anything of value to be buried in the ground. If my heart can save someone, take it. If my liver can save someone, use it. Kidneys, lungs, eyes, and anything else—use them to save someone, but don't bury them."

"I paused for a second, and continued, 'This church has an opportunity to be an organ donor. You can give what's valuable and useful in this church to River Valley, and we can use it to grow and thrive. Your heart is in this church. Give it to us, and the church will live and reach this city. It will be your heart, but it will be beating in the chest of River Valley Church. Don't bury all God has done in your church."[3]

The man who had been so angry and defiant looked around the room and almost laughed. He said, "I say we vote right now!' And they did. Of the 40 people present, 36 voted for the proposal to become one of our campuses, two voted against it, and two abstained. That night the Post-It note on the map became a River Valley Campus! Today, that campus is home to more than 450 attendees

River Valley's next campus was birthed in a similar way. Southbridge Assembly, was a thriving church of 250 people in Shakopee, Minnesota. The church was pastored by Darin Poli. Poli and Ketterling had attended Bible college together, a few decades before. They were pastors in the same region and were friends. Poli and Ketterling began to talk about the idea of joining forces. Southbridge Assembly voted to give up their identity so that they could be fully adopted as a River Valley Campus.

Poli resigned as the Lead Pastor of Southbridge and became the Executive Pastor of River Valley Church. Today the campus at Shakopee has more than 2,000 people in attendance every weekend. Even as that 'adoption' was happening in Shakopee, another church in the district was also in the process of becoming a campus.

Mound Assembly of God, located in Minnetrista, Minnesota had dwindled to only 12 people. In cooperation again with the Minnesota District, this church was eventually persuaded to also become an 'organ donor.'

"As God brought these things together at the same time, we started to say to our church, 'this year we are giving birth to twins,'" Ketterling said. Two campuses were born at the same time. This happened a second time as the Burnsville Campus and the Edina Campus were also launched in the same year as campuses number five and six were started. Today the campus in Edina has more than 1,500 in attendance each weekend.

CULTURE AND KINGDOM
So what makes the River Valley campuses unique? "**Our goal is to make it feel like a franchise. Everything at every location looks and feels the same. Same brand colors. Same style and approach. Same message. Same children's programs and youth ministry. They are designed to feel the same, but that does not make them all equal in expression,**" Ketterling said.

"There are restaurant chains that are franchises with several different expressions. For instance, Chili's is the full expression of the restaurant. But if you go to one in an airport, you will eat at a Chili's Too. The menu is not as full, but the food and experience is the same there as well."

River Valley's buildings are all designed to look similar. Most of the buildings have a warehouse look. Some have been converted from a traditional church building to look more like the other spaces in the campus family. Some of the buildings are leased, some are owned, but all have the same branding and flow.

One of the defining marks of the River Valley family of campuses **is its commitment to missions** and to generosity. River Valley launched its annual Kingdom Builders Campaign before it launched any additional campuses. Kingdom Builders is an over-and-above giving campaign toward initiatives that expand the Kingdom both locally and globally. Those who attend River Valley give over and above their tithes to support these works.

This campaign has enabled River Valley to raise and give away more than six million dollars every year. The monies raised in these annual campaigns have enabled River Valley to birth campuses, buy and renovate buildings, plant additional General Council churches, support Assemblies of God missionaries and projects, and send some of their church family to the mission field.

River Valley now has eight campuses, with more than 10,000 people who attend every weekend. But they have not just birthed campuses, they have also invested in planting churches. Sometimes they have sent financial support. Other times they have sent key staff to plant self-governing General Council churches in Eagan and Northfield, Minnesota, as well as in Salt Lake City, Utah, Milwaukee, Wisconsin, and Indianapolis, Indiana.

The church that was planted in Eagan, Minnesota, eventually chose to come back into the River Valley family and became a campus. This location has more than 500 in attendance every weekend. The Eagan Campus has now been joined by a Minneapolis City Campus, and a campus in Woodbury.

"Our vision is to eventually have twelve campuses in the metro area. Then, we hope to establish a beachhead church in another world-class USA city, and attempt to duplicate the same thing in another place. Can you imagine if we could plant 12 additional campuses in another state, functioning in the same way we do here in Minneapolis," Ketterling said. "We want to plant more campuses, continue to send and help more churches to be planted, and continue to send more missionaries as well. In fact, our goal is to send 500 missionaries from our church into global missions. The goal to send missionaries has slowed our ability to plant more churches, but we have now sent 139 individuals from our church to be foreign missionaries as well."

Ketterling stated very emphatically, "River Valley is for planting churches everywhere. We want to see more campuses, more churches, and more global missionaries. One of the keys for us has been our partnership with our district. We decided early on that we wanted to be a larger church that was leading the way in working with the district. We give to district campaigns, send kids to camps and conventions, serve on committees, and try to serve our district in any way possible. I need to model what it is to be under authority, which means to work toward the goals of those in district leadership. If I want people to work under my authority, I need to show that I am a man who works under authority as well."

CORE IDEA

An Attractional/Video Venue Multi-Campus Church operates by the principle that high quality, effective ministry will flourish in whatever community it is planted. Therefore, the goal is to reproduce as exact a duplicate as possible. The brand is essential. The teaching must be the same. The worship is the same in essence and quality. The kids, youth, groups, and other departmental ministries carry the same approach and DNA.

This requires component management and highly effective decentralized structure and leadership. It also means that there must be regular inspections and constant improvement.

KEY QUESTIONS

1. What does each entity/location have in common?

Every campus has as much in common as they possibly can manage because it is designed to be the same.

- The teaching/preaching is the same person, about 80% by video.

- The music is the same (although other Attractional Model churches allow for a variation in style depending on the community and the culture).

- The branding for what is published, broadcast, and produced on social media is identical.

- The staffing structure is the same at all locations, although bigger campuses might have a few more staff members than others.

- The governance is the same—meaning one board and one executive leadership team.
- The budget and financial management that serves all locations is identical.
- The approach to missions (Kingdom Builders) is the same and all campuses give financially and send teams toward the same overall projects.
- In many Attractional Model Churches, even the buildings and architecture are designed to look the same.
- Special events, such as conferences and dinners, are held in a way that every campus can participate.

2. What is customized?

What might be customized has to do with the personality of the local campus leadership. Each campus does take on a little bit of the vibe of the Campus Pastor and the community that surrounds it, but not so much as to override the DNA of the larger organization.

3. What is centralized?

Attractional/Video Venue Model Churches require the highest degree of centralized horsepower to keep the quality levels at each location strong.

- Financial Management
- Communications
- Service Programming
- Teaching/Preaching
- Social Media
- Worship Leader Development
- Conferences and Events
- Ministry Program Design & Development
- Growth Track Design

- IT & Technology
- Web Hosting and Design

4. What are the pros of this model?

This model has the potential to build the largest crowds and grow the fastest because the quality and effectiveness produced in a new area gains immediate traction in a new community. In fact, many times there are people from a given community who are traveling longer distances to attend a highly effective attractional church.

Great leaders who do not feel a strong call to preach weekly or lead their own church, can serve as Campus Pastors. This role gives them a place to lead hundreds and even thousands of people while focusing on their area of strengths—which tends to be pastoral care, team building, leadership development, and the execution of a plan.

One of the hidden pros of this Attractional/Video Venue Model is the high potential for giving toward projects that benefit the Kingdom of God in the local region and around the world. Many of these churches, although attractional, are also highly missional in the way that they mobilize people and resources.

5. What are the cons or limitations of this model?

Very few leaders are able to lead an Attractional Video Venue Church. It's typically led by a pastor with a unique and specialized combination of gifts: excellent communication skills, strong leadership courage, a high commitment to excellence, and effectiveness in creating systems for distance management.

Typically, this approach to ministry requires significant financial capital and the ability to continually raise up and recruit high-level talent to serve each location.

My observation is that this model thrives best in suburban areas where there are multiple communities that are somewhat similar in demographics.

6. What are the start-up and ongoing cost factors?

Typically, the Attractional/Video Venue Model is the most expensive to start and maintain. First, there is the cost of renting or leasing space large enough to handle the expected crowds. Second, there is the need to hire enough staff to be able to produce the level of quality to meet the expectation. Then, there is the cost of equipment to make the broadcast of the message possible.

Of course, the expectation is that after the launch, the giving will kick in for that local campus expression. Normally, the size of the campus will provide the support needed for ongoing staffing and facility maintenance. Just like when you buy a house, it comes with expenses. So it is with launching a location.

7. What is the level of management competence needed to provide proper controls?

Again, the Attractional/Video Venue Model tends to be the highest on the need for management competence and quality controls. There must be enough centralized staff to support the function of the campuses. Every location has to buy into the overall vision and values in order for the brand to properly carry to each community.

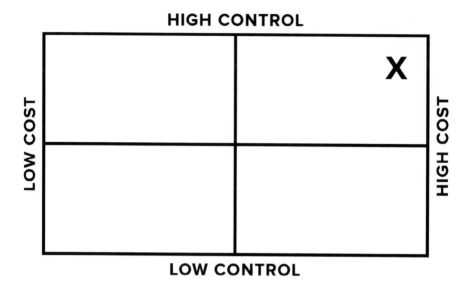

HIGH CONTROL

X

LOW COST | **HIGH COST**

LOW CONTROL

EXAMPLE CHURCHES

- River Valley Church - rivervalley.org
- James River Assembly - jamesriver.church
- Northpoint Church - northpointchurch.tv

NEXT STEPS: What should I do if this is the model that I want to pursue?

1. Explore attractional/venue churches and watch their services online and get a feel for the style and approach to ministry.
2. Visit several of these churches and check out the kids areas, and visit several locations.
3. Consider attending the River Valley Conference to meet their team and get exposure to their philosophy of ministry.
4. Build a budget and determine what it will take to launch a video venue campus.

5. Identify a neighboring community that has a similar demographic as the one where your church is located. Research how many people currently drive from that community to attend your church.

6. Start to drive through that community praying for direction from God and looking for potential venues.

MODEL #2:
THE EMPOWERMENT/LIVE
SPEAKING MODEL

Some transitions in leadership are just more intim-idating than others! When a new pastor succeeds someone who has built a great church and pastored it for years, the challenge can be overwhelming. Pastor Rod Loy served as the Kid's Pastor, then as the Executive Pastor under Pastor Alton Garrison at First Assembly in North Little Rock, Arkansas. Then in 2001, when Pastor Garrison became the District Superintendent of the Arkansas District, Pastor Loy was elected to succeed him.

At that time, North Little Rock was one of the leading churches in the Assemblies of God, and was several thousand in number. There was only one location (as most churches in 2001 had not yet discovered multisite). This church was known for its effectiveness in evangelism and discipleship.

When Pastor Loy stepped into this intimidating role, he determined to do it with his own style, gifting, and approach to ministry. His relaxed demeanor, along with his attitude of honor made the transition into leadership both natural and sensible in every way.

ENTRY INTO MULTI-SITE

"Really early in the game our local Assemblies of God Section had supported church planters in some of the towns that needed new churches," said Loy. "One of those plants was in Volonia, Arkansas. For whatever reason, that plant was unsuccessful. Some were beginning to conclude that towns like Volonia were just too difficult to reach. For me, that was a signal that God was telling me to plant right there in that very difficult place!"

Loy began his search for a church planter by looking at the Arkansas District minster's list. After a season of prayer he felt prompted to talk to Pastor Jim King, who was pastoring a leading church in Booneville, Arkansas. Loy invited Jim and his wife, along with the District Superintendent, Alton Garrison to meet.

"How would you like to come to pastor nobody with me?" was Loy's recruiting pitch. To his surprise, King said, "Yes." and then added, "God told my wife this morning what this meeting was about. We both felt that we were to say 'yes.' So yes, I am in!"

The goal was to effectively plant a church in Volonia, a town of 5,000 people, and make it a General Council (self-governing church). But after pastoring for a season, King made a request of Loy. "**We don't want to become a General Council Church. We feel that we can do more and be better together.**" Loy agreed and this led the leadership at First Assembly to begin researching the concept of multisite ministry.

Now, 17 years later, First Assembly Volonia remains a strong campus that still belongs to the First Assembly family of campuses.

THE VALUES

This first attempt at multi-campus ministry in Volonia has now led to First Assembly, becoming one church in 11 physical locations, with a very large online campus as well. The emergence of this movement was really less about the model of multi-site and much more about some very deeply held values.

#1 - Go to the Difficult Places

"I am sort of a contrarian," declared Loy. "I had no interest in looking for the upwardly mobile suburb, where we could plant a fast growing location or church. My desire is to buy when everyone else is selling. So we started to look for the rural towns or urban areas that desperately needed a breakthrough. We want to run into places where no one else wants to go."

"There is really no grand strategy," said Loy. "We feel called to the overlooked and ignored places. There are places where there should be a church, and there just isn't one. For instance, everyone was moving out of Helena, but we felt we needed to go there. We are the only church in the entire county"

#2 - Seek Influence Not Control

In this model, every campus is given a large amount of autonomy but is invited to choose to participate with the larger whole to gain resources and momentum in what they do. "It is not an expansion model to build the brand," explains Loy. "It is a needs-based model. Where is a church needed? What do we need to provide for that church to succeed?"

- Each campus pastor preaches live at their location but utilizes the message materials that Pastor Loy provides for their benefit. Loy writes the messages 10 to 12 weeks in advance, fully manuscripted so they have plenty of time to study and adapt it.

- Each location has a style that fits the context of the community that they serve.

- Many of the campuses maintain their own name and brand. Seven are called 'First Assembly,' but the others have names like: Graceland Church, Hope Church, Station Church, and Metro Worship Center.

- Three are in states other than Arkansas and retain their own district identity as well.

- Two are locations that are under their own district supervision, as well as being connected with the First Assembly family of campuses This means that the governance for the local church is handled at the district level, but the function of the church is more influenced by the DNA and leadership of First Assembly and its family of campuses.

#3 - Resource With Excellence

First Assembly works to provide excellent materials for each location to use.

- All the campuses use the same growth and learning tracks.

- Children's curriculum is based on the messages Loy writes, so that the entire family, in every location can be learning together. "We want to spark spiritual conversations in the home," said Loy.

#4 - Connect Through Relationships

"I am a relational leader," shared Loy. "I tell my campus pastors that if you need something, just call me and we will figure it out. We are not highly structured, however, after three campuses we realized that we needed more systems in place to make it all work together. We are caught somewhere in between a relational permission-giving model, and a systemic structure."

"These campus pastors are my friends. We meet together on Mondays, have lunch together, and do Zoom calls. It has made my life rich in so many ways."

WORKING WITH DISTRICTS

First Assembly has a wide variety of locations. It should be noted that they have seven churches that have been launched in the nation of Cameroon. However, the majority of the campuses are in Arkansas. There are several locations in rural towns. Several in urban areas. One is in a retirement community.

"Our campus in the retirement community is located in the largest gated community in the USA," Loy said. "A church was there previously, but closed. My superintendent told me, "We have a building there. If you plant there, we will give it to you." So Hot Springs Village became the spot for another First Assembly campus.

The Arkansas District and the First Assembly family of campuses, have a history of active cooperation.

- In the first plant, Superintendent Garrison was a key in recruiting the church planter and celebrating the success of the work.

- When the campus was planted in Helena, the District Superintendent worked with Pastor Loy to interview planters, pray over the community, and meet with the leaders in that city. The district donated the land, the building, and about $250,000 to begin the work there.

- One of the campuses planted by First Assembly was a merger with an existing church. It is in the Tennessee District, and the location included $25 million in assets. Before the church merged with First Assembly North Little Rock, the Tennessee District asked Loy to sign a Memorandum of Understanding committing to eventually release this church to become a General Council Church within the Tennessee District. Loy enthusiastically agreed.

- First Assembly has similar agreements with the Assemblies of God districts and superintendents in both New York and North Texas.

"I gain nothing from working in these other states," explained Loy. "But partnering together with these districts brings tremendous 'kingdom gains!' We are going to be obedient to the Lord as He provides the places, planters, and resources. We are going to be obedient to partner and plant as God opens the doors for us."

These efforts to build the kingdom of God have caused the church to grow in every way. When Loy became the pastor, there were about 1,500 in attendance at First Assembly in North Little Rock. Today, there are more than 3,000 in attendance at that original location. Combined, all of the 11 locations average more than 5,000 a weekend, with the Online Campus truly reaching tens of thousands through the broadcast.

Truly God has favored First Assembly as it has been willing to give itself away to reach these overlooked places.

```
┌─────────────────────────────┐
│                             │
│                             │
│       C O R E   I D E A     │
│                             │
│                             │
└─────────────────────────────┘
```

The Empowerment/Live Speaking Model operates by the principle that pastors and campuses who are resourced, empowered, and connected weekly function better together than they would if they functioned on their own. Every Campus has a degree of freedom to design programming based on campus size, community demographics, and current needs. Each Campus pastor is offered the support of the larger central organization and the leadership of the spiritual dad/mom and leader of the entire organization.

Coaching is also provided to department heads and a leadership pipeline is developed to assist the staffing needs of each location. Some expectation is placed on the campus and campus pastors to participate in events and strategies that build community and momentum with the larger whole. This is balanced with some degree of liberty to function in a way that fits the unique vision of the local campus pastor as well.

KEY QUESTIONS

1. What does each entity/location have in common?

In the Empowerment/Live Speaking Model there is a continuum that must be defined that establishes what every location must practice or establish that is common to all locations, and what every location has the liberty to establish according to their own vision or approach. Here's the list of potential conversations:

- Sermon - Is it the same (written in community)?
- Programming

- Location/Church Name
- Branding
- Worship Style
- Youth and Kids Ministries
- Ministry Departments
- Staffing Structure
- Weekly Announcements
- Events, Conferences, etc.

2. What is customized?

Again, the Empowerment/Live Speaking Model uses the same above listed to determine which of these are able to be customized to the particular community and location.

3. What is centralized?

Most often, in this model there is a degree of central support provided.

- Governance is most often centralized. There is one board that oversees the entire movement of campuses. Some churches make sure that there is representation from each campus on the board.

- Financials are often centralized with one set of books and each location is represented within those books with its own budget and cost-center.

- Depending on how much is common to all the campuses there might be centralized program-ming, sermon planning, social media, communica-tions, video production, events, conferences, and more.

- Most often there is some type of coaching pro-vided to kids staff, youth staff, and other key ministry staff so that each location is developing competence in those areas.

4. What are the pros of this model?

Most of the positives that we see from this model comes from the word 'empowerment.' There is something very attractive about belonging to something larger and yet having a degree of freedom to be yourself and receive the coaching to become even better. This liberty in style and approach also gives a multi-campus church the ability to reach many different types of communities. Rather than producing 'clones,' there is more freedom to do what might be most effective in reaching a specific culture or demographic.

There is also an argument that could be made that allowing campus pastors the opportunity to speak more regularly, will contribute to the development of a great number of effective communicators. That also means that, potentially, the organization becomes less dependent on that one key leader and his/her communication and leadership gifts.

5. What are the cons or limitations of this model?

With freedom comes the potential for a reduction in quality. It is possible that one poorly functioning campus can damage the brand of the entire movement of campuses. If someone visits campus 'A' and has a positive experience, and then later visits campus 'B' (with the same name) and has a sloppy or poor experience, they might walk away with a low opinion of the entire church.

If leaders are not purposeful to define what the DNA (common values) are, this model can feel a bit chaotic—where everyone just does their own thing. To function at the highest level, there must be some level of buy in as to what makes the multi-site movement unique and special, and as to what needs to be guarded and protected

6. What are the start-up and ongoing cost factors?

The costs can vary depending on the vision and philosophy of the overall church. It is possible to start some locations without a lot of investment. If a meeting place is available, and the demand for common programming is not high, a campus could begin with a unique approach and strategy.

It is also possible for the Empowerment/Live Speaking Model to invest just as much capital into the launch of a new campus as the Attractional/Video Venue Model would. The only variation being that they would have a live speaker rather than video teaching.

7. What is the level of management competence needed to provide proper controls?

Again, there is a continuum with this. If leaders of a multi-campus church decide they want a highly protected brand with most of the ministries and programming in common, they would have just as much centralized controls as would the Attractional/Video Venue Model.

But if the Empowerment/Live Speaking Model allows for higher levels of freedom, there is less need for regular centralized management and control.

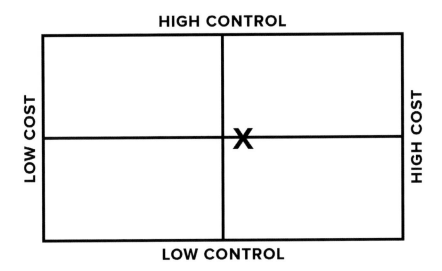

EXAMPLE CHURCHES

- First Assembly Little Rock - Rod Loy - firstnlr.com
- One Church - Kyle & Marcia Bethke - onechurch.com
- New Hope Church - Jeffery Portmann - newhopech.com
- Christian Faith Center - Monty Sears - experience-cfc.com

NEXT STEPS: What should I take if this is the model that I want to pursue?

1. Explore Empowerment/Live Preaching Mode, watch their services online, and get a feel for the style and approach to ministry.

2. Select a church to visit. Go to several of their locations and check out the welcome area, the kids' areas, and the way the service is run.

3. Interview one of the Campus Pastors and ask about his/ her perspective on the benefits and the frustrations of this model.

4. Start to pray over a map of your area. Ask God to give you discernment about where the needs are in your region.

5. Start to meet with pastors who are discouraged and whose churches are struggling. Take them to lunch. Be an encouragement.

6. See what the Lord does as you look to serve the Kingdom.

MODEL #3:
THE MICRO-CHURCH MODEL

Matt and Lindsay Nelson started in ministry together in their early twenties. Three years after joining the team at North Church, in Oklahoma City, the church was growing rapidly. As they were fasting and praying about accepting their future, the Nelsons felt an inner stirring that now was the time for them to plant a church.

They resigned and went to Tulsa, to work with a very good friend to establish this new church. The plan was that it would be a team approach, but Matt and Lindsay would take the lead role in the church planting process.

"Looking back, the structure of this arrangement was not a good idea," Matt Nelson said.. "I would not recommend it. It was messy. It was difficult. The team we had assembled started to fall apart. But somehow in the midst of all of that God started to move. Miracles were happening. People were coming to Christ."

It was the best of times and the worst of times, as they say. One couple on the team went through a marital struggle and got divorced. Six months into the plant, Matt made the difficult decision to release the very friend who had recruited him! Then, another core couple had their marriage fall apart. In some ways, the pre-launch was a total disaster. But in other ways, there was great favor on the Nelsons and their team. "We were out on the streets winning people to Christ. We were seeing many burned out believers returning to church. It was incredible," explained Nelson.

The church launched in 2010, in the middle of the worst ice storm in Oklahoma history. But despite the less than ideal day for their grand opening and the relational storms that their launch team was going through, they were able to push through. Eighteen months later, toward the end of 2011, the church started to hit its stride in both health and growth.

From the very beginning, it was Nelson's desire to create a culture that was designed to love and serve the city. That's why they chose the name City Church. God had also put it in their hearts to be a 'sending church' that would make disciples, send out leaders, and multiply.

"Early on I found others who were planting churches, and we tried to help them. We gave finances, made a place for them in relationship, and tried to assist them in any way that we could. In the first few years, we worked alongside six or seven church planters," Nelson recalled.

Based on the momentum that was growing out of this vision, in 2017 Nelson started Seed Network: a network with the vision to plant 100 churches in 10 years by planting national and international churches. The Seed Network began with international launches, in partnership with Nelson's good friend, missionary Stephen Keurt. Together, Nelson, City Church, and Keurt planted fourteen new churches in Kenya and Burundi and also launched a church planting school with the intention to put 200 new churches in 200 quadrants in east Africa.

Seed Network also worked to launch seventeen new churches in the USA, all planted with the focus of helping these works become autonomous self-governing churches. These were churches, not City Church campuses. City Church developed two pathways for planters.

1. **Relational Cohort** – Church planters are invited into a cohort where the Seed Network coaches them, does life with them, and invests in them as leaders. Men's and couple's retreats were designed as the method to connect and equip these pastoral leaders and their spouses.

2. **Residency** - Potential church planters are invited to join the team at City Church for six months to a year where they can serve, absorb the DNA of the church, and be mentored and prepared to launch a new church.

These new church planters are encouraged to attend the CMN Network's Launch event to complete their training. About 40% of the church plants are started with the Parent Affiliated Church (PAC) status, as a daughter church to City Church Tulsa. Typically, they remain as a PAC for the first two years, then are encouraged to become autonomous and self-governing. The remaining 60% of the churches planted are not looking for official covering, but simply want a 'tribe' of relationships with which to connect.

As of last year, City Church, in partnership with the Seed Network, launched a second campus location as well. The original location is in Midtown and averages approximately 750 people each weekend. The second location, planted in 2019, is located in City West and has about 120 people attending on a weekend. Both campuses are located in low-income and often forgotten areas of the city.

The dynamic between City Church Midtown and City Church West is like many multisite churches: there is one budget and one board. Each Campus Pastor speaks live every weekend (no video teaching) and operates with a unique style and approach to ministry.

MICROSITES AND THE DISCIPLESHIP DNA

Within the last year, there has been a big shift in the strategy and approach to multiplication "We have always had a desire to be innovative and have been willing to try new things," said Nelson. "I had the opportunity to connect with some leaders who have been a part of disciple-making movements around the world. These leaders, from both South Africa and India, have impacted millions of people through their movements. Their model for ministry began to influence our thinking and approach."

"We began to ask the question: How do we make disciples in Tulsa, of people who don't attend church and are not even interested?" Nelson said. "Unless we take the gospel to them they may not hear or respond. Most people who live in Tulsa are not interested in a traditional method of evangelism, like an Easter production. The reality is that 70% who live in Tulsa are not attending any church, so if we are going to reach them, we are going to have to do something differently."

The AG Trust celebrated this innovation in one of its recent emails:

"We believe every single person is called to GO, and is a missionary sent to reach their city, their friends, and their places of influence," says Pastor Matt Nelson.

City Church's micro churches have reached out to the community by operating in these areas of need: foster care, public schools, neighborhoods, CrossFit gyms, homelessness, revitalizing of communities, coaching sports, domestic violence victims, marriage mentoring, retirement homes, and people struggling with addiction. Twice a year the church has hosted **Love Tulsa Sunday**, where they canceled Sunday services and sent their people all over the city to love and serve people, often in places where the micro churches had already been investing each week.

When people new to City Church attend the Growth Track classes, they are asked what ultimately connected them to the church. The number one response has been that they were attracted to a church willing to cancel its services to go and love their city. They also said that Love Tulsa Sunday was the catalyst for them meeting people in the church and getting connected to the community and a micro-church.[4]

"We believe that the gospel moves most naturally through someone's pre-existing social network, said Nelson. "So we are training people to reach their own sphere of influence, like coffee shops and gyms. We want to assist people to take the gospel as the solution to areas of brokenness in the people who are right within their own sphere of daily function."

The goal of this new model is decentralization. The primary focus is on equipping leaders to lead their own microsite somewhere within their natural flow of life. The primary training is on how to win people to Christ and then pastor them in some type of group setting. The steps are as follows:

- **Preparation** – Three-to-four people, as a team, begin praying about where to go.
- **Activation** – Each of these team members begin to engage in making disciples and leading a discovery group.

- **Acceleration** – As people are reached and the group grows, the focus shifts to planning for multiplication, as these groups tend to multiply rapidly.

- **Connection** - Some who attend these microsites attend a City Church Campus every week, in addition to their microsite, while others might only attend a City Church Campus once a month.

"Our goal in planting microsites is not necessarily to grow City Church," explained Nelson. "It's to grow the Kingdom. It's possible that as our microsites multiply, the second and third generations might not be connected to City Church in any way."

These microsites are truly released to form their own strategy. They meet on whatever schedule the leader determines. The locations are typically hubs of activity like a gym or a coffee shop. In many ways, the microsites could be described as not quite an autonomous church and yet much more robust than a typical small group.

Nelson described this difference, "Most small groups focus on building community for those who attend a larger church. When you focus on 'community' you may or may not get missional! But when you focus on 'mission', you always get community. Microsites are not as much about how close can you get relationally but about reaching the city and making disciples."

Matt and Lindsay host their own microchurch in the public school, where their kids attend, in addition to pastoring City Church Midtown. Currently, City Church has trained and mobilized 15 microchurches and hopes to launch an additional 15 to 30 in the next year.

"The goal is to plant microchurches in our city and to plant churches around the world," states Nelson. In fact, if you look at the walls at the Midtown Campus auditorium, you will see on the right wall, the vision of planting churches around the world through the Seed Network and on the left wall, the vision to plant micro-churches in Tulsa.

HOW MICRO-CHURCH IS DIFFERENT

Pastor Nelson declares, "The tragedy of the church today is that we are quite content watching a "rock star" pastor or a talented few use their gifts at the expense of thousands of unused gifts sitting in the seats each week."

The City Church philosophy of ministry is based on the following concepts:

- Our greatest asset is not the few gifted pastors and staff, nor the buildings and programs, but it is the people of God living on mission!

- We want people to choose their church not based on the Sunday gathering, where they look to find a place to meet their needs and preferences. We want people to choose a church based on their capacity to own a shared mission of spreading the gospel to places where it has not yet effectively arrived.

- We measure success not so much by butts in the seats or money given to programs, but by disciple-makers released and new microchurches started.

- We believe that the Sunday gathering is for equipping, encouraging, and inspiring people to GO, rather than the main event where people come to receive ministry.

- We believe that loving and serving the community is not an interruption, nor is it optional but is essential to the life of every follower of Christ. Therefore we want loving and serving the community and living on mission to be priorities that are integrated into the daily rhythm of life.

- We believe that church finances should be used for the maximum kingdom benefit and not so much spent on better Sunday production, nicer facilities, and more programs.

- We believe that all efforts of the body of Christ should be focused on planting churches, meeting the needs of the city and the world, and obeying the Lord. Therefore, the systems and programs that exist in our church should help us love others, make disciples, and reach the unreached.

City Church's Kingdom Vision for Tulsa

Mission: to see our city and the world transformed by the gospel of Jesus Christ.

Strategy: to raise up disciples who are making disciples, living missionally, and bringing the kingdom of God to all areas of our city through micro-churches.

Vision for the next 10 years (2020-2030):

- To see 100,000 people reached and discipled in Tulsa and the surrounding area through micro-churches

- To see 2,000 micro-churches launched

CITY CENTRAL: (Macro-church) City Central exists to empower, equip, and resource the micro-church into deeper levels of mission and disciple making. What support does City Central provide for micro-church planters?

- **Training** - Initial training that helps a micro-church planter get started, build a team, and move towards disciple-making.

- **Coaching** - City Central will provide each micro-church planter a coach to encourage, direct, shepherd, and provide accountability along the way.

- **Sunday Hub** - A Hub is a City Church Sunday location that exists to surround each micro-church planter with a system of support and encouragement.
- **Resources** - We are committed to exhausting every possible resource at our disposal to help our micro-church leaders succeed. This may include, but is not limited to, media resources, finances, facilities, etc.

CITY HUBS: Hubs are once a week Sunday gatherings located in strategic places around our city where we gather to be encouraged, trained, and inspired into mission. What happens at a City Hub?

- We create space for worship, prayer, and coming to the table through communion.
- We share stories of what God is doing in our city and around the world.
- We equip people to live out the gospel.

MICRO-CHURCHES: A community of people gathered around a common mission, to make disciples and to bring the kingdom of God to all areas of our city. What happens in a micro-church?

- A team is formed around a common mission in our city (a cause, place, people, etc.)
  - They commit to pray and look for opportunities to love, serve, and engage in spiritual conversations.
  - They work through a Discovery Study, an obedience-based Bible study that leads to a deeper understanding of God.

- The team is then sent out to make new disciples with the goal that these new disciples will begin new micro-churches.

What is required to be a micro-church planter within the City Church network?

- Alignment with our Kingdom Foundations and Kingdom Culture

- Commitment to a City Church Hub and coach

- Assemble a micro-church disciple-making team (minimum four people committed to a common mission)

- Micro-church minimum requirements: meet regularly, establish a common mission emphasis, actively make disciples, work towards micro-church multiplication

What is required to start a micro-church in the City Church network?

- Complete the Micro-church leader application online or attend a Discovery Night

- Begin monthly coaching meetings

- Acquire training/skills through online resources
  Connect with a micro-church coach to walk through the process

- Upon approval as a micro-church planter by City Church leadership, attend a weekend retreat to prepare for the three phases of a Micro-Church

```
┌─────────────────────────────────────┐
│                                     │
│                                     │
│          C O R E   I D E A          │
│                                     │
│                                     │
└─────────────────────────────────────┘
```

The Micro-church Model, is based on the models of the fast grow-ing disciple-making movements around the world rather than the megachurch models popular in the USA, and operates by the principle that every single person is called to GO as a missionary, sent to reach their city, their friends, and their places of influence.

KEY QUESTIONS

1. What does each entity/location have in common?

Each Micro-church has a common purpose and inten-tion to penetrate the leader's pre-existing social network with the gospel and to see the people reached, not only become followers of Jesus, but be raised up to eventu-ally launch their own Micro-church.

2. What is customized?

Everything about the Micro-church is customized, from where they meet, to when, to how long, to what they choose to do when they gather.

3. What is centralized?

The training process for every Micro-church leader is the same, as well as the process for launching their group. Currently, new believers also go through the same Growth Track training. Every Micro-church is also invited to participate in common outreach projects.

4. What are the pros of this model?

The primary pro is the focus on evangelism and the abil-ity for anyone to enter the process of multiplication and become a Micro-church leader. The concept is that there is the possibility for almost anyone to carry this vision and execute the plan. This is the key to exponential growth around the world, and hoped for here in the USA.

5. What are the cons or limitations of this model?

There has not been a long track record of Micro-church movements in western affluent countries. In addition, decentralization on a massive scale is often difficult to manage. It can be challenging to track what these entities are doing and if they continue to carry the values and effectiveness into the future.

6. What are the start-up and ongoing cost factors?

This Micro-church Model has the lowest cost of any of the models, which is another huge pro. There is little cost for salaries, facilities, or operations.

7. What is the level of management competence needed to provide proper controls?

At first, the level of management is fairly simple. It merely involves excellence in recruitment, training, and coaching. But eventually, it begins to become more complex as layers of coaching need to be built into the process to ensure Micro-church leaders are healthy, growing, cared for, and executing the values.

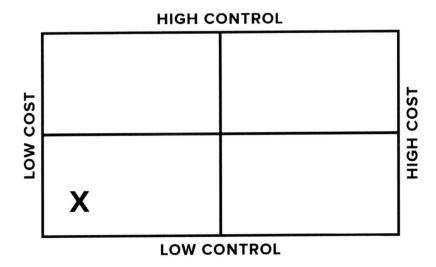

EXAMPLE CHURCHES

- City Church Tulsa - Matt Nelson - <u>citychurchtulsa.com/</u>
- Parklawn Church - Bishop Walter Harvey - nbfag.org/reach-25/
- Bishop Harvey is leading an initiative with the National Black Fellowship to plant churches in urban areas with the microchurch model as their primary strategy for reaching neighborhoods within cities.
- Dinner Church Collective - (see dinnerchurch.com) - The Dinner Church Collective is a nation-wide community of mealtime missionaries spreading the word about a simple, effective and historic approach to starting new forms of church.

NEXT STEPS: What should I do if this is the model that I want to pursue?

1. Explore the Micro-church Model by visiting the church and attending a Hub Gathering or Leader Training.

2. Personally start a Micro-church in your community and learn by doing.

3. Start to pray over a map of your area. Ask God to give you discernment about where the needs are in your region.

4. Begin to write out your step-by-step philosophy of ministry as to how to equip your first few microchurch pilot projects.

MODEL #4:
THE CIRCUIT RIDER MODEL

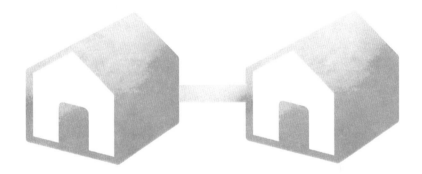

One of the ways that Christianity spread rapidly across the continent of North America was a strategy employed by the Methodists to reach frontier towns and villages. They sent out spiritual leaders, called 'circuit riders' as they often would travel on horseback, to serve anywhere from 25-30 different communities at a time.

These were the early church planters of their era. Francis Asbury was one of the most famous of these missionary pastors. It is estimated that he may have traveled as many as 270,000 miles in his ministry career, planting churches in village after village.

Pastor Denny Curran, of River of Life Church in Cold Spring, Minnesota, is a modern day example of the circuit rider model. While he does not travel on horseback, his passion for the rural areas of Minnesota has prompted him to plant churches in a way that harkens back to the methods of the 1700s.

Curran was saved back in 1971, in his early 20s. "I started to get into trouble at the age of 15 years old, using drugs and alcohol and acting out in ways related to that." Curran stated that he had five choices,"1) Join the armed forces (during the era of the Vietnam war) 2) run away to a place like Boulder, Colorado to find myself 3) go deeper into drugs 4) commit suicide, or 5) give my life to Christ."

"One night, I was in my bedroom and I prayed, 'God if you are real, show up in my life. I will go anywhere you want and do anything you want. I will surrender!' remembered Curran. "As soon as I said that I felt God physically enter my room. It shook me so much that I ran into my bathroom and I locked the door. So I prayed again, 'God, if you will get out of my bedroom, I promise that I will follow through on what I just prayed!'"

"Had I known that that would mean full-time ministry, I might not have prayed that prayer! I was afraid God was going to steal all my fun, or send me on some remote missions assignment." The first step Denny took, however, was to join a traveling Christian singing group. They asked him to join, not for his voice, but for his testimony. They would sing. Denny would tell his story. "I later found out that they had my microphone turned off every time we sang!"

Some of those that were discipling Denny encouraged him to enroll at North Central University. He went, intending only to learn more about his faith, and to get a degree. Curran recalls, "I had no idea that this was an Assemblies of God school, or even what the Assemblies of God was! Honesty, I was not planning on going into ministry, but rather to travel with a professional softball team."

"Just before I left school, I got down on my knees," said Curran. "I prayed: I don't want to be in the ministry, but if you will show me what you want me to do God, I will do it." When Curran got up from his prayer time, he walked out of the building and bumped into the President of the school, E.M. Clark. Clark asked him to consider doing an internship at an Assemblies of God church in Paynesville, Minnesota and soon, arrangements were being made. While Denny started as an intern in Paynesville in 1975, he eventually became the Lead Pastor in 1985.

THE PLANT IN COLD SPRING

For several years Denny did everything he could to grow the church. When the church did grow, the older members would get upset. They resisted anything or anyone new, even those who were getting saved. "I was getting depressed, and feeling trapped," remembered Curran. "I said to my wife, 'I want to start something on my own and build on a healthy foundation, not on the foundation that someone else has built.'"

This discontent in Curran began in the 1990s, which was the beginning of a nation-wide initiative in the Assemblies of God, to believe that the final 10 years in the millennium would be a 'Decade of Harvest.' Denny took it upon himself to help to launch a new church in the town of Cold Spring, located twenty miles away from Painsville. On Tuesday nights, he would travel to Cold Spring and hold a Bible study for a small group of people at the Riverside Inn. On Sundays, he would pastor and preach to the church in Paynesville.

This effort to start a new church invoked opposition from every direction. An influential local leader opposed it and worked to scatter the twelve faithful people attending the Bible study in Cold Spring. Curran's board and people at the church in Paynesville opposed it, objecting to him spending his time on this new project. But the Superintendent of Minnesota, Clarence St Johns, continued to encourage Denny to plant.

Eventually, the church in Paynesville forced him to choose. Curran would either leave to pastor the new work in Cold Spring, or he would give up the Cold Spring plant, and focus solely on the Paynesville church. Denny and his wife Cheryl decided to resign from the Paynesville Church and launch the new church plant in the town of Cold Spring.

Curran said, "In Paynesville, I was leaving a prime piece of property, with 150 acres, and a building that was debt free to go to the town of Cold Spring with a population of only 2,975 people. At the same time that I was making this decision to step out in faith and leave a steady salary and job, my father was offering me some capital to start a company with him. But after a few days away, in fasting and prayer God spoke to me. I was praying at a retreat center, and on the way out, someone said to me, 'Never forget this! Jesus is all you need!' At first, I was like, 'How does that help me right now?' Then the Holy Spirit stamped that in my spirit. He is all I need. He will take care of everything that I need."

On January 12th, 1994, the Curran's relaunched the Bible study in Cold Spring with 12 people. After a few months, they moved the service from a Tuesday night to a Saturday night and 44 people showed up. Momentum continued and now, 26 years later, there are more than 800 who attend River of Life Church. Imagine that, 800 people in a town of only 3,000!

PASTORING TWO CHURCHES AT ONCE

The pattern the Currans started in Cold Spring has now been something that they have done six more times.

In fact, after only six months in Cold Spring, some people in the neighboring town of Glenwood called and asked Denny to plant in their area. But at the first interest meeting, the idea of a new church in Glenwood, planted in a new way, to reach new people, was not at all met with enthusiasm.

"I talked about how a seed has to fall to the ground and die, in order to produce a harvest," explained Curran. "The people in this meeting understood that some of the old ways of doing church would not work in a new church plant. So almost all of them just walked out!" There were only a few willing people left in the room. Curran chose to plant this new church in Glenwood with the few.

Tuesday nights in Glenwood were Bible study nights. Sunday mornings in Cold Springs, Curran pastored his newly planted church. After a few months, Denny cast vision to a group of pastors in that area. He invited them to share in the joy of planting a new church. Instead of excitement, this idea was met with resistance. "Give me one good reason why we should plant a new church in Glenwood," voiced one of the older pastors in the room. Finally, another pastor stood and said, "Give me one good reason why we should not plant a new church in Glenwood."

This pastoral group of leaders decided to approve the new church and for a season, the Currans served as the pastors for these two churches. Eventually, through a series of divine appointments, God provided a space in an old high school building. The owner of the building, touched by Denny's vision for the community, allowed them to rent the space for only $10 a month. Soon a new pastor was identified to lead the Glenwood church, allowing Pastor Denny and his team at River of Life to slowly transition the church to become a self-governing church.

The church in Glenwood eventually grew to be over 300 people on a weekend, in a town that is a population of only 2,500! "In this model, it usually takes between twelve-to-twenty-four months for a church to become strong enough and healthy enough to govern itself," said Curran.

After the Glenwood church was established, the Currans used the same method to plant new churches in Freeport, Becker, Sartell, Annadale and Pelican Rapids. The Waters Church in Sartell has also become a rapidly multiplying church and has now planted 10 new churches in its short lifetime. Think about the chain reaction of the Curran's obedience and faith. One church plants another, that plants another. This is what true movements are!

In every situation, God has used the Currans willingness to personally go into new territory in rural areas and do whatever is necessary to begin a new work, even though it has meant needing to pastor two places at the same time.

```
┌─────────────────────────────────────┐
│                                     │
│                                     │
│          C O R E   I D E A          │
│                                     │
│                                     │
└─────────────────────────────────────┘
```

The Circuit Rider Model operates by the principle that it is possible to pastor two locations at the same time, for a season, to reach a new town for Christ. It also recognizes the reality that it is difficult to recruit planters into rural towns without any visible sign that a sustainable church can be birthed there. By pastoring two locations at once, momentum can be created without having a planter from the beginning. This makes it possible to raise up a pastor from within or to recruit someone from outside who might see the vision more clearly once the new church has become established.

1. What does each entity/location have in common?

The primary thing that each location has in common is the actual lead pastor for the first few months or years of the new church's existence. This allows the DNA of the parent church to be deeply embedded because the pastor is able to establish that themselves.

2. What is customized?

Every aspect of the new church is able to be customized for the community, including the facility in which they meet and the eventual pastor that will lead the new church. It is also possible to make both churches very similar. This decision about how similar the locations and churches become is truly up to the local leadership.

3. What is centralized?

At the beginning everything is centralized. The larger, more established church is providing everything for the newer emerging church. Often the worship leader is leading at both locations, and many of the leaders at the parent church might be serving at the church plant, as well. Accounting, social media, communications, programming, and all planning is driven by the lead pastor at the established parent church.

Over time, more and more of these centralized systems of support are assumed by the newer church plant until that new location becomes fully autonomous with its own budget, books, board, and ministry development.

4. What are the pros of this model?

This approach maximizes resources. It builds on something and someone who has demonstrated the ability to provide healthy ministry. It has a lower cost since it uses the same staff and resources for both churches at the beginning of the new launch.

5. What are the cons or limitations of this model?

If not practiced carefully, there is the potential for burnout for both the lead pastor and the team from the sending church. There is also the danger of draining too much talent leadership and ending up with two smaller, weaker churches in the long-run. It's important that at least one, if not both, of these locations continue to aggressively grow by reaching new people for Christ and creating a leadership and talent pipeline.

6. What are the start-up and ongoing cost factors?

Costs tend to be low because of shared staff and resources. The biggest cost, at the beginning, tends to be renting a space and marketing the location.

7. What is the level of management competence needed to provide proper controls?

The need for management competence is often low simply because the Lead Pastor is actually doing most of the leading personally at both spaces. The type of competence that is needed is more pastoral effectiveness than it is management competence. Once a new pastor is recruited for the new church, management for the new location is then released to the new leader.

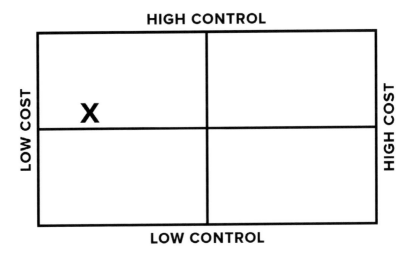

EXAMPLE CHURCHES

- River of Life Church - Denny Curran - riveroflifeag. org
- https://www.ruralpastors.com/
- Cornerstone Church - Stand Saunders - cornerstonechurch.cc
- (While Cornerstone church is not an exact Circuit Rider Model, it does have similarities because of the commitment to planting campuses in rural locations.)

NEXT STEPS: What should I do if this is the model that I want to pursue?

1. Start to pray over a map and consider towns and communities that need a new church.
2. Drive through those places and pray.

3. Host an outreach in a community of need to see the response and look for God's hand at work in the area.

4. Consider starting a small group to meet and pray in that community.

5. Study other churches who plant in rural areas or use this Circuit Rider Model.

MODEL #5:
THE INTERNATIONAL VENUE MODEL

CASE STUDY

**EVANGEL CHURCH
PASTOR RON HEITMAN**

After spending 12 years as the District Youth Director in the Illinois District of the Assemblies of God, Ron Heitman and his wife, Tamra, were invited to candidate for the role of Lead Pastor at Evangel Church.

"This great church was like a burnt over field, that had known seasons of incredible fruitfulness," described Heitman. "When a farmer has produced a great crop, and there is left over stubble, they will often burn the field to remove the obstacles to future harvest."

God called Ron and Tamra to lead this church into a new season of plowing, planting, cultivating, and harvesting. Multiplication was a part of this church's DNA and history from its inception. But the church had become barren for a season. The vision for new churches had to be reignited.

THE INTERNATIONAL VENUE

One of the things that became apparent to the Heitmans was the international dimension of pastoring in Chicago. "I started to track the number of different nations represented in our congregation, and we began to mark each nation by a flag that we hung in our auditorium. At last count, I think we have 60 nations represented. It's a beautiful picture of the body of Christ,' described Heitman. "And also presents to us a unique opportunity for multiplication."

"One day as I was praying in our chapel, a smaller venue in the Evangel building, God spoke to me about a FULL CAPACITY VISION," explained Heitman. "During this moment of prayer, God birthed a dream to see different language groups reached through specific venues designed to reach them. I was given a vision for both an Indian congregation and a Spanish one as well."

"I picked up the phone to call my friend Pastor Wilfredo (Choco) De Jesus, (a fellow multi-site pastor in the Chicagoland area, and shared my vision," said Heitman. "Pastor Choco said to me, 'I think the chapel would be perfect!'" Within six months, Hetiman had launched two new 'campus venues' in the chapel, right within the Evangel Church building.

When Heitman first arrived at Evangel Church, they had two services but had to move to one. After a few months in their first attempt to multiply, they began a second service and learned the skills of reproducing leaders in every area of the church: kids ministry, worship, and hospitality.

When Heitman launched the language-specific venues, he launched them at the same time as the English-speaking services. The Indian service was at 9:00 a.m. in the chapel, while the English-speaking service was meeting in the auditorium. Then at 11:00 a.m., the Spanish-speaking service met in the chapel, while the English-speaking service operated their second service in the auditorium.

"We have found that one of the big wins with this method is that all of the venues utilize the same kids and youth ministries. The international congregations love the idea that their children are going to church with English-speaking Americans. They want their kids to be assimilating into the American culture. In fact, a barrier to sustaining a language-specific church into the next generation is that often the kids of those in the first generation don't want to stay in that language-specific congregation. Often when those students mature they will leave their language specific church for an English speaking church."

God provided some key miracles in connecting Heitman with the right leaders for the language specific venues. A sovereign set of events led Heitman to meet Austin Albertaj. Albertraj had planted churches in the region of Madras, under the leadership of Dr. David Mohan, but had since immigrated to the USA and planted an Indian church in Chicago. Heitman had given to Dr. Mohan's effort in India to help their multiplying church and because of his financial partnership with this healthy leader and church, felt great confidence upon meeting Austin. Heitman presented the idea of joining forces to launch a new venue at Evangel Church.

For Albertraj this fed his passion to multiply. He used his existing church that met in the afternoons to help Heitman start the new Indian service in the Evangel chapel at 9 am reaching a whole new group of people.

After starting the Spanish venue, God then provided a Spanish-speaking pastor, from within Evangel Church. These pastors had already been attending Evangel, and eventually were raised up to become the Campus Pastors of this new venue.

Most recently, Evangel Church planted a Mongolian campus. One of the largest populations of Mongolians, in the USA, resides in the Chicago Midwest area. God sovereignly brought a Mongolian family who had previously planted a church in the capital city of Mongolia, Alaanbaater. Together, with Evangel Church, this pastor planted the first Mongolian Assemblies of God Church in the United States. "What's amazing is that this is truly a missional venture," said Heitman. "Most Mongolians are totally unreached. They are Atheists or Buddhists, and are totally unaware of Christianity and its worldview!"

To make room for this new campus/venue, Evangel Church had to do some renovations, knocking out a wall, to make several smaller rooms into a larger one. After several months of meeting as a small group, this new Mongolian congregation began to meet in the renovated space.

Currently there are only 16 Mongolian churches, of any denomination, in the entire USA. This new congregation at Evangel Church is being used by God. Not too long ago, they hosted a conference for leaders that flew in from all around the country representing these 16 Mongolian churches.

NEW DISTRICT POSITION
Ron's experience in the District Office as District Youth Director, and his track record for planting these international congregations,

led to the Illinois District creating a new position that he now fills. Ginger Kolbaba, described this transition in the AG News:

Today, Evangel Church has birthed multiple parent-affiliated churches (PACS), including Indian, Hispanic, and the first Mongolian AG congregation in the U.S. Evangel Church is in the process of planting Russian, Polish, and Japanese congregations.

"The need is so great," Heitman says. "We must multiply to reach lost people."

His passion for evangelizing the lost garnered the attention of the Illinois District. In June 2017, seeing the urgency to help make such outreach happen around the state, district officials voted to add a second assistant district superintendent position. The district hired Heitman, whose sole focus in the role is to oversee church multiplication in the eight counties that make up Chicagoland.

"We wanted Ron to take the experience he has with planting and growing PACs and share that with other church leaders," says Illinois District Superintendent Phil B. Schneider. "We have the largest immigrant area in our nation. So who better to choose than a man who is already feeling that burden and God's call?"

Heitman took on the role with enthusiasm, but with a caveat. He wouldn't forsake his pastoral post.

"I felt like the Lord wanted me to come alongside other pastors from a position of strength as a fellow pastor," says Heitman. "That way we can truly multiply churches together."

The district agreed, breaking down his role as 40 percent assistant superintendent work and 60 percent pastoral work. In Heitman's first year, the district already has seen results. One of his responsibilities involved putting together a team to help lead the campaign to multiply healthy churches, and then to set a strategy for moving forward.

"We want to empower church-planting churches to create new church plants," says Schneider. "Ron has already made great strides with that." Schneider points out that 5 percent of the AG churches in the district are less than five years old. A total of 10 new churches are expected to be launched in the area this year.

Although there are a total of 100 AG churches in greater Chicago, Heitman is eager for more to open. His vision is to see every one of the 77 Chicago city neighborhoods have a vibrant AG church. That's 300 different zip codes.

"The world is literally at our doorstep," Heitman says. "With the Lord's help, I believe we will see a healthy church reaching people for Christ in every zip code."[5]

FROM VENUES TO LOCATIONS

In the last few years, Evangel has now launched a second physical campus location. This campus is focused on modeling the Hanover Park campus with English speaking and translating into Russian to reach both Russian and Ukrainian people. As is the case in each of the other venues, each Campus Pastor speaks live, but uses the outline created by Pastor Heitman. This second location has opened up a brand new vision for Evangel Church.

"Our dream is to see more locations established, but to have each location house multiple ethnic and language-specific services," said Heitman. "Each congregation could share not only facilities, but also the staffing for children's and youth ministry."

Why multiply in this way? Heitman said clearly, "It's not because it is easy, that's for certain! There is a significant cultural gap that has to be continually bridged. It requires tons of patience with each other and cultural intelligence. We have developed a motto between us, when there is a difference. We say, 'It's not wrong, it's just different!'" One technique that the staff has utilized to bridge the gap, is to have each Campus Pastor share during staff meetings about the uniqueness of their culture.

FROM PLANTERS TO PARENTS

What's Heitman's current dream for Chicagoland? In the last few years, there have been 12 new churches planted. "Now, our focus is not only on recruiting church planters, but also on developing more multiplying pastors," said Heitman. "We need more influential churches that want to become parent churches, who are willing to multiply to reach these new areas for Christ."

"In the parable of the talents, in Luke 19, when God gives us a talent, he intends for us to multiply what we have been given," Heitman said. "Some churches are capable of multiplying 10 times over. Other churches are capable of multiplying five times over. But the church that chooses to bury their potential, out of fear, will eventually lose whatever they have been given."

The focus of the Chicagoland vision is all about healthy churches that can multiply. As they do, they will fulfill the promise of Isaiah 54:2-3…

"Enlarge the place of your tent, stretch your tent curtains wide, do not hold back; lengthen your cords, strengthen your stakes. For you will spread out to the right and to the left; your descendants will dispossess the nations and settle in their desolate cities." The New Living Translation translates that last sentence as "For you will soon be bursting at the seams. Your descendants will occupy other nations and resettle the ruined cities."

Heitman recalled, "The day I was elected to this role as Assistant Superintendent, Scott Hagan, the President of North Central University, gave me a prophetic word. He said, 'If you will walk among the ruins, I will do in days what has not been done in decades.'"

```
┌─────────────────────────────────────┐
│                                      │
│                                      │
│          C O R E   I D E A           │
│                                      │
│                                      │
└─────────────────────────────────────┘
```

The International Venue Model operates by the principle that one of the greatest opportunities for a harvest of souls and the establishment of new churches is found within the various pockets of immigrant and ethnic populations in our cities. Providing a parent organization as well as functional facility space and even shared ministries, offers a level of strength of support and momentum that these new venues/congregations can leverage for the Kingdom.

1. What does each entity/location have in common?

We call this model a "venue" because it implies the use of a common space. One facility with many congregations that potentially can meet in various spaces throughout that building(s). That is the only essential thing that the organizations share.

Some churches might have their International Venue Churches share a common brand with their parent congregation. Others will not. Some might preach the same sermon outlines in their own language. Others will not. Some will have central governance. Others will not.

Evangel Church offers each international congregation the ability to share the same children's ministry programs, as most of the children can function completely in an English-speaking environment.

2. What is customized?

Typically, the language, worship, style, and approach to the services are customized completely to fit the culture. Everything is customized in an International Venue except that which the parent church indicates the two congregations must have in common.

3. What is centralized?

Again, the only essential centralized feature is the facility. Everything else must be defined, determined, and negotiated between the parent church and international venue congregation.

4. What are the pros of this model?

The benefits of this model are many: Cost Effectiveness, because the same facility is used more than once. More effective community reach, because some people will not come to a church if they do not understand the language or can't relate to the culture of the parent church. Strength of Community, because international pastors often feel alone and without real connection and support. Diversity, because the parent church now is able to branch out beyond their primary demographics.

5. What are the cons or limitations of this model?

The biggest challenge can be the sharing of space. Sharing space often requires patience, agreement, and constant communication. Sometimes one group can feel taken advantage of by the other. Second, there are cultural differences in communication, style, and approaches to leadership.

It takes time and intentional effort to bridge those cultural gaps. Finally, there is the limitation of longevity. Often, language-based churches do not live past one or two generations because the children of those families prefer to attend an English-speaking church once they have assimilated to American culture. Consistent evangelism of first generation language speaking people is necessary.

6. What are the start-up and ongoing cost factors?

This is one of the greatest benefits to this model of multiplication is that the only cost might be to outfit a room in the church with the equipment necessary to host an effective service.

A potential downside to having multiple congregations using the same auditorium is navigating through the decisions of which congregation will be meeting at less than optimal times during the week.

7. What is the level of management competence needed to provide proper controls?

Most of the competence comes in the area of managing the facility, the schedule, the expectations, and the execution of services between all these various congregations. There is also the need to develop cross-cultural management and communication skills if all of these congregations come under one centralized organization.

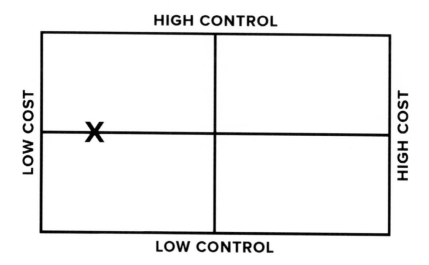

EXAMPLE CHURCHES

- Evangel Church - Pastor Ron Heitman - evangelchurch.cc
- Cityreach Church Philadelphia - Pastor Mark Novales - cityreachchurch.net

NEXT STEPS: What should I do if this is the model that I want to pursue?

1. Do some demographic research on your community to identify communities of immigrants or refugees.
2. Start to pray that God would connect you to a leader/pastor who could launch a ministry to reach a unique ethnic community.
3. Begin to strategize how your facilities could be used to begin a new venue.
4. Visit and study a church who has an international, ethnic, or language service.

MODEL #6:
THE MERGER/REVITALIZATION MODEL

CASE STUDY

**FIRST ASSEMBLY OF
GOD VICTORVILLE
PASTOR JOHN C. MARTIN**

When we think of what is needed for more healthy
local churches across our nation, we tend to think in two categories. First, we think of new churches, locations (campuses) and
venues. Traditionally, we would call that 'church planting.' Second,
we think in terms of revitalizing churches that have either pla-
teaued or declined.

The multi-site ministry model can offer a way to make both of these objectives happen at the same time. Locations that have been in decline can potentially be renewed as a new campus is launched under the auspices of a healthy local church.

This is what is happening through the partnership between the Southern California Network and the ministry of Pastor John C. Martin and First Assembly of God.

THE MOVE TO VICTORVILLE

On September 10, 2006, Pastor Martin was elected to be the pastor of First Assembly in Victorville, California in the county of San Bernardino. Victorville First had gone through many problems, and accepting the assignment as Lead Pastor was something that the Martins had to pray through because they recognized this transition was going to be more challenging than their previous churches.

But with an assignment from God comes a special grace from God for those specific challenges, and First Assembly began to see many people come to Christ. "Someone has been saved in our church every week for the 14 years we have been here," said Martin. "And as new people get saved, the entire culture starts to change for the good. This is what happened during the first 12-24 months. The church started to grow, new people were being saved, and the past was being restored for the people of Victorville First."

Two years into this season of healing, salvation, and revitalization, Superintendent Ray Rachels (then the leader of the Southern California Network) called Martin about some churches in crisis that were in neighboring communities to Victorville. "John, I need some help," explained Rachels. "You've got two churches in your backyard going through pastoral transitions. They border your town. Would you be willing to do this new thing called 'parenting' and bring these two works under your oversight of Victorville First?"

Martin said, "I remember this as if it was yesterday! I was taken back by the opportunity, and after some prayer, we said 'yes.'"

Apple Valley became the first mult-isite location for Victorville First. The pastor, who was 80 years old, was retiring. The church had dwindled in numbers and the members were not able to pay the salary for a new pastor. So Martin made Apple Valley a campus and placed an associate pastor there and soon the church began to grow again.

Nine months later, Victorville First added the Hesperia Campus. Again, they identified a Campus Pastor that would relocate to Hesperia, and with new leadership and some healthy DNA deposited in the church's culture, this second campus also began to grow.

"These steps to adopt these churches started to change me as a pastor. It started to change us as a church. We began to dream about starting and adopting many more campuses in the future," said Martin.

Currently, Victorville First Assembly has now rescued seven churches, in partnership with the Southern California Network. The term 'rescue' is very specific because this vision for one church to 'rescue by adoption and parenting' has become a vital part, not only of the vision of Victorville First, but also of the Southern California Network. "Our Superintendents, both Rachels and now Rich Guerra, have had a belief in our ability to both plant and to rescue, and their faith in us has made all the difference," declared Martin.

In addition to their seven 'rescue' locations are six newly planted campuses as well. Now Victorville First has 13 locations! "Our goal is to plant or rescue a church/campus every year until Jesus

comes," declared Martin. "When we plant a new location, we purpose to go to a community of need and plant a campus there.
When we rescue a church and transition it to a campus, we wait
for the Southern California Network to ask us to be involved. We
have never intentionally gone after a pre-existing church, we
always wait to be asked."

THE VICTORVILLE APPROACH

Every one of the 13 Victorville campuses have live preaching.
"I have nothing against video preaching," explained Martin. "I
realize that I am now 57 years old. Rather than build the ministry
around my communication gifts, I feel a call to raise up 20 pastors in the next 20 years. The only way to fully raise them up is to
release them to preach."

Every week, Martin leads a Zoom call with his pastors where they
talk through both the sermon series and the preaching strategies.
At quarterly one day meetings, they design the preaching content for the upcoming four-to-six months as well as discuss issues
unique to each campus. Once a year, they take a retreat together
to plan, set goals, and strategize.

The other thing that is unique about the Victorville approach is
that any campus is free to leave the multisite family at any time
to become a General Council Church, provided they meet the
required criteria. So far none of the campuses has left the Parent
Church because each one seems to appreciate the advantage
and value of remaining a Parent Affiliated Church.

If a location wants to be released to be an Assemblies of God
General Council church, they must meet the following criteria:

1. Strong leadership must be in place. Each location needs
   a pastor, a capable board and solid lay leadership.
2. Quality ministry to all age levels. The campus must provide quality ministry for the adults, youth, and children.

3. Minimum of 50 members. The larger the congregation, the better chance for sustainability and health.

4. Demonstrate financial stability. For a location to be released, they must be financially in the black for at least one year.

Another unique feature to the Victorville approach is that they do not insist on the same brand. Each location has its own name. Victorville is called First Assembly as are most of the campuses. But the Tustin location is called Legacy Church. The Azusa location is called Canyon City Church.

"It's interesting to see how over the course of time, we have widened the tent," explained Martin. "We don't require the new campuses to be an exact version of us. Some towns are not huge communities. With the goal of a healthy church in every town, we put churches in places where the church may never be more than 100 people, and that's okay. They don't have to look just like us in style, name, or approach. So we often name them according to the town where they are located rather than the name of our church. We are writing the book as we go and things change every time we learn something new."

All 13 of these Victorville campuses are governed centrally. All the funds go into one central account, and the campus pastors receive monthly financial reports specific to their location.

To aid in the governance process, some campuses have local members serving on advisory teams that help provide input to the pastor for that local situation. This also helps to cultivate future board members for the larger entity, because campuses are training and investing in these leaders on a regular basis.

Every member at every location is invited to the Annual Meeting each year. They attend this meeting at the campus location they normally attend and cast their vote, for decisions being made that affect the whole network.

The combined overall attendance of these 13 campuses is now more than 3,700. The original Victorville First location has grown from about 1,000 to more than 2,300 since Martin became the pastor. The Apple Valley Campus is now about 500. Some locations have 50 and others 250.

PHILOSOPHY

"Let's put lots of hooks in the water and go fishing. If we catch trout, great. If we catch halibut, great. Let's see what God brings us and put the resources toward whatever God is blessing." We have become incredibly diverse which led us to offer services in English, Spanish, Sign, Korean, and Indonesian languages."

"We want to be a multi-ethnic, multi-generational, multisite church," said Martin. "Saying 'yes' to God is a huge phrase for us. If you sense God is in it, then say 'yes' and you will figure out what God wants to do in the midst of it all. This has been our process, to trust God and believe that He was going to do something through us."

"Because we saw early success in the steps we had taken to rescue churches, we were transformed to believe we could do more," said Martin. "Having district leaders that believe in us makes all the difference."

```
┌─────────────────────────────────┐
│                                 │
│                                 │
│          C O R E   I D E A      │
│                                 │
│                                 │
└─────────────────────────────────┘
```

The Merger Model operates by the principle that sometimes the best method of revitalization is to have a parent church adopt a failed or dying location and intentionally rescue and replant a vibrant life-giving church or campus. If a parent church is effective as a multi-campus or church planting church, it can transfer those skills to a dying or dead location and impart to that church a healthy culture and growing DNA. If successful, this strategy becomes a benefit to the parent church, the rescued church, the district, and the Kingdom of God.

1. What does each entity/location have in common?

When a parent church adopts a location the goal is to impart as much healthy DNA as is possible at the beginning. This requires that the adopted location joyfully adopts as much of the language, values, strategy, and schedule of the parent organization. Typically, the new locations will accept the parent church brand, governance, accounting systems, and ministry programs and plans.

2. What is customized?

Depending on the vision of the parent organization, some degree of flexibility and customization may be afforded to the adopted location. Each of these customized liberties should be negotiated and defined in advance. This might include keeping the name/brand of the adopted location. It might also include the freedom to program services or preach messages, continue with programs or plans that were working and effective within the community.

3. What is centralized?

Almost always governance and accounting is centralized, at least for a season, to get the adopted location healthy in every way. Things like programming, service planning, scheduling, events, and ministry departments might be centralized or customized depending on the multi-campus philosophy of the parent church. In some cases, the teaching/preaching might shift to a video venue. In other cases, live preaching continues where messages are prepared in community.

4. What are the pros of this model?

There are so many benefits to this model:

- Often Assemblies of God Districts have too many dependent churches to oversee and may lack the personnel needed to effectively reboot a location.

- Sometimes the biggest barrier to a revitalization is the pre-existing structure and culture of a failing church. The Merger Model is a benevolent take-over and allows for a total reboot of a dying church.

- The facilities of the dying church can now be repurposed, which is a huge win for the parent church and for the Kingdom of God.

- A parent church that has a multiplicational impulse is given greater capacity to reproduce leaders and locations.

- The community where the dying church is located benefits because a life-giving church is now replanted there.

- The overall Assemblies of God denomination benefits because the Merger Model keeps churches open

5. What are the cons or limitations of this model?

- A parent church could fail in their efforts and make things worse for the adopted location and or the district.

- Donating facilities to larger effective churches could be seen as playing favorites and offering perks to churches that are already succeeding, while churches that are struggling do not receive the same benefits.

- Some might accuse the parent church of 'personal kingdom-building' and/or some parent churches might actually work toward 'personal kingdom-building.'

- Concern that a parent church might absorb all the buildings of failed churches and then leave the denomination or cause problems for the neighboring churches in that region.

6. What are the start-up and ongoing cost factors?

Start-up costs greatly depend on the situation. Some adopted locations may need a lot of renovations. Some parent churches might choose to put money into a location to make it fit the DNA of their approach to ministry. Often there is a need to provide a salary to the campus pastor or church planter. Sometimes, the adopted location brings debts with it that have to be repaid.

7. What is the level of management competence needed to provide proper controls?

Typically, the level of management competence is fairly high, at least in the short-term. The ability to reboot a church/campus in a different community requires healthy intervention, communication, and oversight. Things will not get better without intentional effort put into building relationships, teaching values, training staff and volunteers, and so much more.

The long-term management competence is dependent on whether the parent church intends to keep the location as a permanent campus or release it to become an autonomous church, after it becomes healthy again.

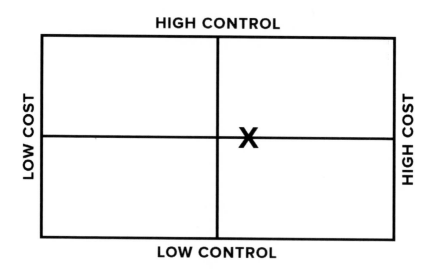

EXAMPLE CHURCHES

- First Assembly of God Victorville - Pastor John C. Martin - vfassembly.org
- New Break Church - Pastor Mike Quinn - new-break.org
- C3 Church - Konan Stephens - myc3church.com
- Bethel Church - Gerad Strong - bethel.ag

NEXT STEPS: What should I do if this is the model that I want to pursue?

1. Begin to actively serve and give to the vision of your district (denomination).

2. Prove yourself to be a team player who is willing to invest in the district leaders where you are located.

3. Start to pray for and encourage pastors who are struggling or discouraged.

4. Look for ways to help other local pastors succeed.

5. Eventually, have a conversation with your local or district leaders about a potential merger/revitalization opportunity.

6. Study how other churches have effectively made this process work.

MODEL #7:
THE CHURCH PLANTING
NETWORK MODEL

CASE STUDY

**ALLISON PARK CHURCH REACH
NORTH EAST INITIATIVE
PASTOR JEFF LEAKE**

This case study is fairly easy for me to describe as it is the story of my own journey with church planting through the efforts of Allison Park Church (APC). As I explained in the introduction to this book, God prompted us to prioritize the needs of our city ahead of the growth of our congregation. We did this through the decision to plant new churches in towns and communities within driving distance from our church.

First, we sent our youth pastor (Pat Summers) to plant Crossway Church in Mars, PA, - which was a twenty-minute drive to the north. Next, we planted in the city of Ambridge, which was a 45-minute drive to the west. Our third plant was in the town of Sharpsburg, PA, which was a 20-minute drive to the southeast of APC.

A trend started to develop. We began planting in small communities along the banks of one of the three rivers in the city of Pittsburgh. These towns had historically been populated by immigrants from Europe who came to the USA to work in the steel industry. When the steel mills closed down in the 1970s, these communities went through numerous economic and community hardships.

Our fourth plant was within the city limits of Pittsburgh, in a region called Bloomfield. Church plant #5 was a 20-minute drive to our southwest in a community called West View. Each of these churches was initially launched as a daughter church. This means that we governed them, and they functioned much like one of our ministry departments with a cost center and budget that was a part of the overall books of Allison Park Church.

The goal, however, was to quickly assist these new churches to become autonomous. We took them through a three phase process.

First, we wanted these church plants to be self-propagating, meaning that they would grow through the efforts of those on their committed team. We allowed the church planter to recruit from APC, but we stipulated that we wanted anyone who went with the church planter to hear from God and be committed to the new church as their home, rather than just making a temporary move.

Second, we wanted the new church to be self-supporting. We invested finances in their launch and expected every church planter to raise additional funds as well. Our goal was to give them a big push so that they would have enough people, leaders, and money on the day of their grand opening to be able to sustain the church out of the giving of their own members within a few months of their initial launch.

This occurred in all five situations! This was the only way that we were able to keep planting so rapidly. Our strategy was dependent on each church staying open, growing, and paying its own bills. We were not built to carry these new churches financially for more than a few months.

The third step was to help the new church become self-governing. The church planter would select and recruit three-to-five trustees. I would sit down with their aspiring board and do a training with them and with the planter on healthy church governance. Once they had enough trustees and enough official members (at least 20) we would fully release them to be an autonomous church.

The fastest this process went was three months! Sharpsburg Family Worship Center was planted by Russ Horne, who had been my associate pastor. Just about 100 people from APC decided to go with Russ and help him plant this new church. God had done a miracle, as well, in providing an old church building in the center of town for only $25,000. Sharpsburg Family Worship Center was autonomous within a few weeks of its launch due to a few additional key factors: Russ was highly competent, this launch was significantly resourced, and Russ and I had a great working relationship and a high level of trust.

The longest this process took was about three years, but we determined that this was too long for the health of the new church and for the momentum of our church planting efforts. So we established the expectation that a new church should become autonomous within the first nine-to-eighteen months after launch.

A NETWORK IS BORN

Once these first five churches were started, I began to notice that some of the planters were in need of encouragement, fellowship, and ongoing resources. I invited them all into a meeting that we held in the back room of a local Panera Bread. Every week, we met for an hour just to laugh, eat, talk strategy, and encourage each other.

Before long, this life-giving gathering attracted the attention of other pastors in the area. Some asked if they could join in for lunch, even though I had not planted them. We said, "YES!" and our group began to grow.

Something else happened as we met together. We decided to plan a week of outreach to each community during the month of August that became a yearly event for a while. This initiative allowed us to mobilize the people of APC (especially the youth) to go on mission and serve our city. During the day, we helped staff a VBS-ike event for each new church plant. During the evenings, we held outdoor events, community parties, and services under a tent.

This desire to serve the community more regularly eventually sparked the idea to birth a non-profit ministry that could help these church plants serve their community. This 501c3 became known as the Network of Hope (NOH). NOH has helped churches start foodbanks, launch support groups like Celebrate Recovery, Grief Share, afterschool programs, and other types of need-based programs.

In 2003, the city of Sharpsburg was damaged by a significant flood. For an entire year the Network of Hope based its outreach in this new church plant and worked as the locally-designated Red Cross relief site to help the community dig out of this damage. Hundreds of thousands of dollar's worth of clothing, furniture, food and other resources were donated through the Network of

Hope to the people of the community. This all happened through the partnership between Allison Park Church, Sharpsburg Family Worship Center, and the newly established Network of Hope.

From 2004 to 2006, Allison Park Church concentrated its focus on raising the money to build a new auditorium and concourse (fellowship space). When that was completed, the decision was made to go back into the business of church planting. Five more churches were planted in the city of Pittsburgh in the succeeding years, in the communities of Tarentum, Lawrenceville, Millvale, the South Side, and Braddock.

When we planted in Braddock it was the first time that we gave birth to a grand-daughter church. Our tenth plant was actually sent out by one of the churches we had previously planted. We shared in the expense and in the joy of seeing this new church established. Now our network had hit the third generation of reproduction, which was to be a foreshadowing of things to come.

FORMALIZING THE NETWORK AND THE VISION

Somewhere in the journey toward our tenth plant, we felt the need to make our church planting network into something more formal. We formed a 501c3 that eventually became known as Reach Northeast, which had the goal of planting churches in the northeastern part of our country.

We also launched a local church ministry school (now called Allison Park Leadership Academy) which was designed to train leaders from the ground up to serve as worship leaders, kids pastors, youth pastors, and even future church planters.

It was just as our church planting network was hitting its stride that God spoke to me a second time about a new wave of church planting. I had been pastoring at Allison Park Church for 20 years, as of 2011. I was doing some soul-searching about what the future was supposed to look like for my ministry. I was asking God what he wanted to do next and began proposing some numeric goals to God. We had done one church a year for the longest time. "How do you feel, Holy Spirit, about 10 churches in 10 years?"

I felt no affirmation on that proposal within my spirit. So I decided to think about what we could do if some of our daughter churches started to plant as well. So I proposed to the Lord, "What about 20 churches in 10 years?" Again, no affirmation or peace inside.

Now, I should say that I believe wholeheartedly in doing things out of discernment. God still speaks. When we set goals, we often can do so out of human strategy or personal hubris. When we do things based on a word from God it lifts us into a new dimension of breakthrough in our lives.

God moves in responses to our obedience and faith! For me, it has always been about that. What has God said? How can I obey? What are my next steps of faith? I believe the entire concept of reproduction is based on that partnership.

Back to the story. When I proposed to God the goal of 20 churches in 10 years, I felt no affirmation from Him. So I asked, "God, what is it that You want to do?" To which I immediately heard the Holy Spirit whisper..."100!"

I then argued with God! "No way. That's too large. It's impossible." But I could not escape the sense that was burning inside that He wanted me to believe for 100 new churches in 10 years. When I shared it with my wife, she said, "Wow. Yes. I sense that too." Actually, I was hoping for some reasonable person out there would talk me out of this seemingly crazy revelation but every leader that I shared this with in my process of gaining buy-in, had the exact same response!

In fact, some said, "I knew you were going to say 100 before the words came out of your mouth!" God was obviously doing something wild and bigger than I could have ever imagined.

There is not enough room in this 'case study' to describe all the ins and outs and ups and downs of this journey to plant 100 new churches in 10 years. What I will explain is that we stepped out in faith and started to aggressively plant beginning in 2011. God was faithful and enabled us to reach the goal of starting more than a hundred new churches in the last 10 years. How was that possible?

- First, we started planting churches in clusters rather than just one at a time.

- Each cluster of church planters became a 'class' or 'cohort' of sorts. Instead of coaching the planters individually, we started to coach them as a group. They met together on a conference call every other week. Everyone was working toward the same goals and benchmarks, but they were doing it in community.

- Each cohort or cluster would plant on the same weekend. This created synergy. In 2013, we planted three churches in one day. Two in Boston and one in Binghamton, NY. These three celebrated one another. We measured collective results. It produced a true celebration of the movement to reach the northeast.

- Opening multiple churches in one day created a buzz about what we were doing. Here we were pursuing the dream to plant 100 churches! When word got out that 13 new churches were started in one weekend, it had a way of helping to recruit the next wave of church planters.

- Matching funds were available through several organizations that helped provide the money needed to plant.

- The moment was right. The trend of church planting was hitting its peak around the country right about 2011 and 2012. There were more potential planters than ever that were considering planting.

- Organizations like CMN had honed and developed their launch training. APC would often host one of these training sessions at our location so that we could train our planters and discover more planters that felt a call to plant in the northeast.

One of the initial 10 churches planted by APC and Reach Northeast was CityReach Pittsburgh. CityReach became one of the most prolific multiplying churches in history. For the first few years (from 2010-2014) the churches being planted were healthy, well governed, and sustainable. Almost all of the churches that CityReach planted in the early years, they did in partnership with Reach Northeast. It was two church planting networks working together to plant these clusters.

Sometime during the end of 2014, CityReach and ReachNortheast parted ways, in part over concern about sustainability in planting large volumes of churches at a rapid pace. CityReach was attempting to plant in larger clusters than ever before, all across the nation, with many partners and organizations. Planting churches in such volume came with a degree of fall out. Suffice it to say, it was too many, too fast, with too many partners, and not enough oversight. About half of the City Reach churches planted during the years between 2014 and 2018 were forced to close, often leaving a wake of debt and failed expectations behind.

Many lessons were learned in that era, too many to recount in this simple case study. What I can say is that all the churches planted by Reach Northeast and its daughter churches have remained open and have proven to be sustainable, except for one that was closed due to a personal moral failure on the part of the planter. Half of the CityReach churches remained open as well.

All of this is proof of the fact that multiplication can be messy. Any attempt at multiplication involves risk. No one should tell you that there is not a price to this process! The bigger the assignment from God, the larger the potential for pain. Likewise, the larger the potential for kingdom gain.

Today, Reach Northeast, now called the Allison Park Leadership Network, continues to exist to plant new churches, resource pastors, equip multipliers, and train future church planters and their teams.

```
┌─────────────────────────────────────┐
│                                     │
│                                     │
│           C O R E   I D E A          │
│                                     │
│                                     │
└─────────────────────────────────────┘
```

The Church Planting Network Model operates by the principle that a healthy parent church is the most effective means of planting new autonomous churches that will reach new towns, cities, and regions with the gospel. The goal of a church planting network is not to hold onto locations, and keep them together in a common brand or function, but to release them to form their own vision, brand, function, and uniqueness. This premise is based on the methodology that has made the Assemblies of God (and other international missions organizations) grow rapidly.

This model believes in the indigenous church, where local leadership is raised up to create 1) self-propagating, 2) self-supporting, and 3) self-governing churches.

1. What does each entity/location have in common?

A church planting network multiplies in phases.

- **Pre-launch phase** - The church planter is a part of the parent church and operates within the parent church, and therefore has everything in common with that parent organization, in order to learn the needed skills, embed the DNA, and build relationships.

- **Launch phase** - The church planter launches and begins to determine what about the new church will be unique and what will be the same as their parent church. Most often, the name and strategic language is different. Just as often, there are programs, schedules and plans that remain the same as the parent church

- **Post-launch phase** - After the new church is launched, what the two (parent and plant) have in common is governance. For the first nine-to-eighteen months (some networks go as long as five years) a new church remains under the parent church board and organization. The goal is to get the church strong enough to where it has its own board and governance structure.

- **Autonomous phase** - When the church plant is ready to be released, they become a self-governing and self-supporting organization. Now the primary thing that the parent and the plant have in common is relationship. As sister churches, they may choose to partner together on projects, on planting the next church, on outreaches, on joining in the network's conferences and events. Some networks require a long-term commitment and/or financial support to the parent network that launched them.

2. What is customized?

At first almost everything about the parent and the plant is the same. Eventually, almost everything is customized. It is a journey toward autonomy and full release. Much like a young person who grows up in their parents' house and eventually leaves home to establish their own home and lifestyle.

3. What is centralized?

For the first few phases, financial management and oversight are primarily what is centralized. There might also be some coaching and training to the planter and their team members. Almost everything else is made possible through the efforts of the planter and their launch team.

4. What are the pros of this model?

The pros of this model is that there is a family to belong to as a planter takes the huge risk to launch a new church. With this relationship to the parent church, there is often financial support, the ability to recruit leaders and launch team members, and the sense of blessing and community. There is also a sense of being sent with backing and authority.

5. What are the cons or limitations of this model?

One of the challenges is in the relationship between parent and planter. Often, if expectations are not clearly defined, offenses can arise. Parent churches often feel that their planter does not appreciate what they have been given. Planters often feel that the parent church could have done (or be doing) more to help them.

The other factor that can be a con is the loss of control. That is also a pro, in a way. When a planter is released, the problems that planter encounters goes with them. (Which is not the case when you plant a campus or venue, you keep and have to solve all the problems that continue to arise.)

But when the planter is released, all ability to control the quality, direction, and decisions of the planter are also released. This can be frustrating, especially when things head in a direction that is not healthy nor growing.

Finally, if the planter transitions from the church, the parent church is often left watching a young church struggle without a leader and may not be able to do anything about it.

6. What are the start-up and ongoing cost factors?

The start-up costs are really as high as the parent church chooses. Some parents put in significant amounts of funding (sometimes to match whatever the planter is receiving as a grant from an organization like CMN). But other churches choose only to provide relational and governance support.

There is also the potential costs of the planter recruiting members from the parent church as they form their launch team.

7. What is the level of management competence needed to provide proper controls?

The competence required here is not long-term management skills, but rather start-up management skills. In a multi-campus or multi-venue church you need both the start-up and the long-term management skills. But in a church planting network all that is needed is the entrepreneurial skills to get something off the ground and established.

What is needed long-term is the ability to create a place of ongoing relational safety and resourcing so that the planter feels that they still have a place to belong, get coaching, and be part of a family.

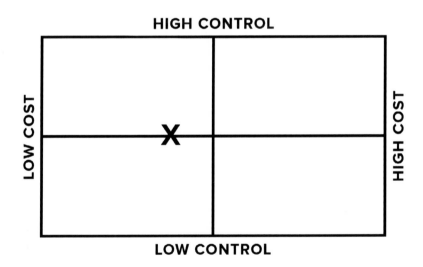

EXAMPLE CHURCHES:

- CityLife Church - Brad Leach - **citylife**philly.com
- Two Rivers Church - Will Hampton - tworivers. church

- Lifehouse Church - Patrick Grach - lifehouse.network/about
- The Waters Church - Doug Vagle - thewaterschurch.net

NEXT STEPS: What should I do if this is the model that I want to pursue?

1. Begin to pray over a map of your region and identify communities that need a life-giving church to be planted.

2. Start to pray for a church planter to be sent into your life (someone with which you can plant).

3. Begin to review and build your leadership pipeline so that you can start to identify potential church planters from your staff or your church.

4. Start to put funds away every month into a church planting fund to get ready for the day when you will, in faith, plant your first church.

5. Consider attending or auditing the CMN Launch Training. Bring some of your staff and/or leaders with you to one of these events.

6. Interview a pastor who has a church planting network to gain better understanding of the steps and approach to planting a new, and eventually autonomous, church.

MODEL #8:
THE RESOURCE NETWORK MODEL

Some pastors just have a way about them that
leaves you feeling welcomed, loved, and encouraged. Pastors
Gabby and Petry Mejia have a 'Barnabas' demeanor about them,
and everything they do in ministry tends to flow from this spirit.

The New Birth Church website describes the planting of this new
church and the vision and passion behind it. "In 2015 God called
our Senior Pastors Gabby and Petry Mejia **to reach and serve the**
lost, hurting and the marginalized in the heart of Kissimmee,

FL – in that, New Birth Church was founded on October 4th, 2015. Through their sacrifice and our leadership teams, New Birth has truly been **a place of hope** by helping serve our communities, having outreaches, feeding and supplying to those who are in need and so much more."[6]

Mejia grew up as a pastor's son in New York City. His father started pastoring there when Gabby was only eight years old, and he is still continuing to serve there, 45 years later. Gabby was raised in the church but had a powerful encounter with Christ on August 18, 1989, when he was 16 years old. At an outdoor youth service, Mejia committed his life to Jesus Christ.

Two years later, Mejia found himself reaching people through the same methods that had reached him. At 18, he became a teenage evangelist, holding his own tent crusades on the streets of New York and New Jersey. Hundreds of young people were saved in those meetings. His ministry also birthed a number of community projects and outreach programs to reach the people living in the city.

In 2000, Gabby and Petry were invited to join the staff of one of the largest Hispanic churches in the USA, Iglesia Calvario in Orlando, Florida. For the next 10 years, they served as youth pastors at this amazing church. But seven years into this journey, God began to speak to Gabby and Petry that one day, they would launch out and plant a church.

When they shared this vision with the Lead Pastor, Pastor Nino Gonzalez, he blessed that desire and immediately encouraged them to act on this impulse from the Holy Spirit. He encouraged them to launch an English-speaking venue within the Spanish-speaking Church, Iglesia Calvario. New Birth was launched in a separate auditorium, and Gabby and Petry began to pastor that church while continuing as the youth pastors.

This arrangement worked amazingly well for a season, but several years into the journey the Mejias felt it was time to establish New Birth Church in its own location. In 2013, they worked with the leadership of Iglesia Calvario to merge the 'English church' with the larger whole. Iglesia Calvario adopted and formally absorbed this work into their church. Gabby and Petry now set their sights to start New Birth Church in a new location.

NEW BIRTH IN A NEW PLACE

The Mejias felt God's call to Kissimmee, Florida. They started New Birth Church in a local high school auditorium there. With just 38 people on their launch team, Mejia knew he would need to find a job to support himself in the early stages of church planting. As he was searching for employment, he discovered a private Christian school that was looking for a Campus Pastor. During the interview, Mejia discovered the school auditorium was available to rent. Gabby not only got the job, this eventually became a second location for New Birth Church!

Now Mejia had a steady income during the first year and with a meeting place that they could afford. But the impulse to multiply is deeply ingrained into the Mejias, so within a year they launched this second location about a 45-minute drive south of Kissimmee. One of the pastoral staff at New Birth felt a burden, so they sent him to this new location with 25 people. Today, this campus has two services with more than 300 in attendance each weekend.

New Birth Church was then one church in two locations, but before the end of 2016, God opened another door of opportunity. Two hours' drive to the west in Port Richey, a church was ready to close. Their numbers were dropping, and that they wanted to give up.

"Everything was so new," said Mejia. "We had no money to invest as a church, and the church in Port Richey was in debt for $30,000. After seven months of praying and discussing our options, we decided to take a major step of faith and go for it. We moved one of our most trusted team members into leadership there. It took about a year to detox the culture and establish our DNA, but eventually the campus started to grow."

The Port Richey location now has two services with more than 300 people every weekend.

New Birth Church is now one church in five locations, reaching several thousand people every weekend. But the multiplication impact of this church, after only five years in existence is now growing in a multi-faceted way. God began to bring in a collection of pastors and churches looking for a covering and a home.

NEW BIRTH PASTORS NETWORK

"In our first year of existence, we experienced unusual momentum in the summer months," shared Mejia. "Typically summer months are down seasons, but we saw 600 people come to Christ that first summer, and broke all kinds of attendance records. So I began sharing about 'how to make your church grow during the summer.'"

Word began to spread and interest grew among pastors of smaller churches in Florida and all along the East Coast. They wanted to learn the New Birth methods of church growth. They also wanted to find a place of safety, encouragement, resourcing and relationship.

"We hosted a gathering of pastors and asked if they would like to join us in a seven-week sermon series," says Mejia. "I would write the messages and design the programming, and they could share in that resource. This is how the network began! We started to resource pastors and churches who did not have the technology or finances to produce videos and special features. They all decided to join in with us on that series."

It was a series designed to create some buzz and keep people connected to their church during that summer season when attendance normally starts to drop. It worked! Now these same churches were ready to follow New Birth Church into additional strategies to grow and reach people.

The New Birth Network is now home to 47 pastors and churches. Some are from small non-denominational churches that have the same doctrine, but have no covering or structure to support what they do. "There is a deep need to belong to something," shared Mejia. "We are meeting that need and providing a place for them."

While most of these network churches are small, some that are larger have also decided to join. "We have one church in Lakeland that has over 1,000 people and another in Aruba that has almost 800 in attendance."

VISION FOR THE FUTURE

Recently, the New Birth Church and Network bought a property in Kissimmee for offices. There is now a Spanish-speaking church (not New Birth) that meets in their office space.

"Our goal for the next 10 years is to plant another 20 churches and to start more New Birth campuses as well," declared Mejia. "Along with that, we want to launch our own school of ministry to train and prepare local young leaders for ministry. Overall, our vision is to be a place of hope!"

```
CORE   IDEA
```

The Resource Network Model operates by the principle that there are countless small rural, ethnic, urban, and suburban churches and pastors out there who are looking for a place to belong. Many of these pastors are looking for a spiritual dad/mom or for some strategic coaching. When a parent church serves as a hub for relationships and resourcing, multiplication happens.

As the smaller churches who join the network become healthier and more connected to an apostolic vision, there is a greater capacity for potential leaders from within these churches to be identified, trained, and released into new churches and locations.

1. What does each entity/location have in common?

The primary way that the Resource Network Model works is to bring pastors and churches into relationship, with the opportunity to join together with common efforts, plans, outreaches, and strategies. It's a unity of desire and shared effort.

2. What is customized?

Since each Network Church chooses off of the menu of resources that the Parent Church provides, everything is customized.

3. What is centralized?

The primary thing that is centralized are the demonstration of and production of plans and resources. The parent church produces something effective (an outreach, a video, a sermon series) and makes it available to the network. There may be coaching provided as to how to use the resource effectively as well.

Network training and connection events, where network pastors can find fathering, coaching, and family, are also centralized

4. What are the pros of this model?

This model is meeting a huge need in the church world by helping churches that might otherwise die, find a way to be healthy and growing. It is very low cost model because the parent church simply make resources they have already invested in available to others

5. What are the cons or limitations of this model?

As the number of churches joining the network grows, it becomes a challenge to provide true personal connection. Eventually, some staff must be hired to service the needs of the network churches or the pastor and staff of the parent church can burn out.

If not purposeful in casting vision, recruiting, and training, very little actual multiplication will happen.

6. What are the start-up and ongoing cost factors?

The start-up costs are very low. Again, the parent church is investing finances in products that they are already using. What could be an ongoing cost is the investment that some network churches might need to survive and start to grow. The only cost described by Mejia is the need to absorb the debt from the buildings they were able to assume ownership over.

7. What is the level of management competence needed to provide proper controls?

Management competence is not a big need in this model. Resourcing, coaching, and spiritual parenting are the biggest needs.

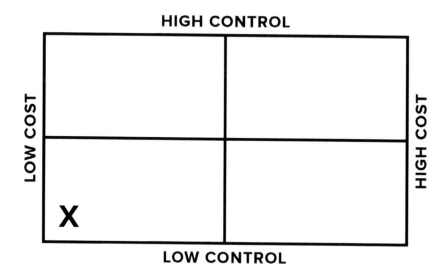

.**EXAMPLE CHURCHES**

- New Birth Church - Pastor Gabby Mejia - http://newsite2.mynewbirth.church

- Northplace Church - Pastor Bryan Jarrett - https://ruraladvancement.com/

- *Jarrett has developed a strategy to adopt 25 rural pastors and churches a year, in order to cele-brate, resource, and revitalize them. Jarrett says, "If someone chooses to go to rural America, in the natural, we want to ask them if they have lost their mind. This is partially because we have not looked at rural America as an unreached people group. People will go to the hard places if they see it in this reframed way. Donors will give to it. Denominations will support it."*

NEXT STEPS: What should I do if this is the model that I want to pursue?

1. Identify resources, strategies, and creative ideas that are working effectively in your ministry

2. Consider how to make those resources available to other churches in a way that will benefit them and their ministries.

3. Identify pastors and leaders in your region that are alone and looking for a place to belong.

4. Meet with these pastors and find ways to encourage them.

5. Identify ways to cooperate on a project or program.

6. Celebrate the wins!

7. See what God does to multiply a network of pastors and churches around you.

MODEL #9:
THE BIG DAY/LARGE LAUNCH MODEL

The story of Radiant Church in Tampa, Florida is truly an extraordinary picture of entrepreneurial leadership, evangelistic passion, multisite excellence, and a harvest of souls. Pastors Aaron and Katie Burke held their first interest meeting in 2013, and today they pastor one church in five locations that has grown to more than 4,000 in weekly attendance.

Radiant Church has been on Outreach Magazine's 100 Fastest Growing Churches list in 2018 (#13), 2019 (#4), and in 2020 (#5).

This rapid growth is based on a model of ministry that Burke established that we will call the BIG DAY MODEL.

One of the things that Pastor Aaron Burke does today, is train potential church planters through the Church Multiplication Network Launch training. He has been one of the key presenters and has trained hundreds of planters around the country over the last few years. He does this because this training, along with training offered by Church of the Highlands and the ARC (Association of Related Churches), was so critical to his success as a planter.

"I went to their Launch event," said Burke. "It was a breath of fresh air. I heard about the success rate for church plants, and the proven approach to marketing and ministry development, and I was absolutely thrilled. I felt that with these tools, I could build a church that we would truly want to attend, where we could raise our family, and where we could impact the community and make a difference around the world."

In 2012, the Burkes resigned from their role as youth pastors at Brownsville Assembly and moved to Tampa, Florida to launch a new church. Why Tampa? "God told me that if I would move there, He would give me the city!'

Aaron joined the Chamber of Commerce in Tampa, visited local businesses, made friends, and with persistence built a launch team. The first interest meeting was held in March of 2013, with 17 adults and eight of those attending officially joined the launch team.

These eight became the workers for the church's first community event. The following Saturday, during a community festival in South Tampa, the team handed out t-shirts and free coffee. "I had met with multiple pastors throughout the community, introducing myself and sharing the vision," explained Burke. "I would ask them, if you were me, where is the biggest need for a life-giving church? Where would you plant? And multiple pastors responded by indicating South Tampa."

This area was known as a 'graveyard' for church planters. The schools were not open to churches meeting in their buildings; It is a landlocked peninsula with more than 100,000 people living within a few miles and it is a wealthy area, the most expensive in all of Tampa Bay.

"We were up for the challenge," said Burke. "We worked to meet people and serve that community for six months. We set a target for the grand opening on September 15, 2013, but could not find a facility to meet in until six weeks before we launched. We found an old 'dollar' theater that was so gross, no one even wanted to watch movies there. The building was more than 50years old. It was disgusting, with stained green carpet and mice. It was rough, but it was the only option."

The lease was signed just in time for the mailer to be sent out. The Radiant Church team worked tirelessly to get the word out in the community and on grand opening Sunday, there were 348 in attendance, with 38 responding to give their life to Christ.

"We knew that God was in it and that we had stumbled into something special," recalled Burke. "The building was raw, gritty, but special. We had to pour bleach down the drain so that no one could smell the sewage. But even in all of that, God blessed that grand opening event."

Over the next six weeks, the church leveled out at about 175 people in regular attendance. That's when Burke began to formulate this BIG DAY model of church multiplication. "I thought, If we did this with a team of only 35 adults on our launch team, what would happen if we did this with 175 people, and launched again in January?" said Burke.

So they followed the same exact plan but with more team members engaged. They strategized and planned on how to engage with friends and with the community to have a BIG DAY on the weekend after MLK weekend in January. When the relaunch weekend came around, they had an even bigger response than in September.

Then Radiant Church took its first step toward multiplication and started a second service. By Easter Sunday, Radiant Church drew 607 people for that holiday. One year from the date of their launch, they were averaging 550 people every week.

"It was then that we realized that multiplication was in our DNA. We imagined that if we relaunched our church multiple times a year, we could multiply services and locations to reach our community in even greater ways," said Burke.

This is when "One Big Sunday" was born:

- 'One Big Sunday' is the branding for this large event, held three times a year.
- All of the Radiant Church outreach and marketing is connected to this big day.
- Everyone is encouraged to invite someone to church with them on "One Big Sunday."

"I say to our people, every Sunday is a good day to bring a friend to church. But for me, I am going to bring all my friends to church on ONE BIG SUNDAY because everything we do that day will be designed just for our visitors. I tell my people who I am inviting, and how many I am personally planning to bring with me to church that day."

THE BIG DAY MODEL

Radiant Church has created a BIG DAY MODEL not only for growth, but also for multiplication. Hosting the ONE BIG SUNDAY event is similar to the evangelistic crusades, held by evangelists over the last few centuries. But it is more than just a crusade, with a special speaker who comes to town, draws a crowd, and then departs. Each "One Big Sunday" is built around a message that the Lead Pastor shares through the regularly scheduled ministry of the local church.

When a friend attends a One Big Sunday, they are actually getting a taste of what they will get if they attend Radiant Church every week. They are introduced to the atmosphere of the church, and listen to the pastor speak a life-giving word into their hearts. Strategically, the message is designed with the goal of preaching the gospel for salvation, but in such a way as to immediately connect with those who have been invited into the local church.

The added benefit of hosting BIG DAYS three times a year, is that, every time a new campus or new service is launched, it happens in combination with a ONE BIG SUNDAY event.

"Our vision and goal is to reach 10,000 people every weekend, through locations all around the city and region, and to do that by our 10th anniversary, which would be September of 2023," said Burke. In Acts 15, the lead elder in the Jerusalem church, James, said, "We do not want to make it difficult for the gentiles who are turning to God." Burke reiterates, in a similar way, we don't want to make it difficult for people in Tampa to find Christ. We actually want to make it difficult for them to go to hell, because we are making it so easy for them to go to church!"

GIVING TOWARD THE VISION

"Every month, we invest finances into three areas of multiplication," explained Burke.

- Giving to **local multiplication** through planting campuses with multiple services.

- Giving to **national multiplication** through organizations like CMN and ARC.

  Radiant Church also pays the salary for two church-planter-in-residency candidates, who are considered part of the staff, so that they can learn and absorb the DNA. When they are ready to plant, the new church planters are sent out with some funds raised in an offering.

- Giving to **international multiplication** by planting churches in India and Sri Lanka. Finances are given to support at least 12 new church planters every year through a Bible school and an apostolic church planting hub.

Radiant Church functions as one church in five locations, in addition to an online campus. All locations are governed centrally, with one board and one budget. Each campus has a Campus Pastor, who speaks occasionally, but the steady diet for the weekend preaching is from Pastor Burke by video.

```
┌─────────────────────────────────────┐
│                                     │
│                                     │
│          C O R E   I D E A          │
│                                     │
│                                     │
└─────────────────────────────────────┘
```

The Big Day/Large Launch Model operates by the principle that if the strategy for holding a 'large launch' grand opening works when you plant a new church, it should continue to work throughout the life of the church to keep it growing and multiplying. A church that uses this model will host a 'BIG DAY' several times a year and through these well planned, big events, seek to launch new services, new venues, new campuses, and even new church plants.

1. What does each entity/location have in common?

The most note-able thing that every location has in common is the push toward the next BIG DAY with marketing, planning, programming, and mobilization of people to invite their friends to attend. Many churches that use this model operate very similarly to the Attractional Video Venue model. However, the key focus is not being a multi-campus, or even video venue, but is in the strategic use of these BIG DAYS.

2. What is customized?

Again, most of these churches will be highly centralized with little customization. What might be customized, in the preparation for a big day launch event might be the way that the event is marketing within the community. The marketing approach may be determined by the demographics of that specific community.

3. What is centralized?

The key to this model is the centralized planning of the Big Day Event and the specific multiplications that will take place on that day. This centralized plan would involve:

- Casting vision
- Creating buzz
- Raising funds for the event
- Programming of the day
- Social media promos
- Marketing campaigns
- Quality control at all locations
- Message planning

What would be executed on-site would be:

- Volunteer team recruitment and mobilization
- Event execution on the days of the events
- Working the marketing plan
- Personal invitations and follow-up

4. What are the pros of this model?

A leader who is skilled at leading a group of people to build a crowd can strategically use these skills not just for the purpose of church growth and evangelism, but also for the purpose of multiplication. Every time there is a BIG DAY Event, it is an opportunity to multiply in some way.

5. What are the cons or limitations of this model?

Some leaders are not skilled at attractional events. Often the cost of marketing can be expensive. Some locations are not robust enough in their development of volunteers and teams to pull off a large and effective event.

If you plan an event and it is a failure, it can be a downer because it has such a high cost in terms of money, energy, and volunteer time. A poor event can cause morale to drop and a leader's credibility to be damaged.

6. What are the start-up and ongoing cost factors?

The cost of events can be high depending on what level you are working toward. Securing facilities, sending mailers, buying food, and making sure you have quality music and programming all has a significant cost to it.

7. What is the level of management competence needed to provide proper controls?

The need for management competence is high for this model to be effective. This is a coordinated effort to make an excellent event happen, often in multiple locations at the same time. There are hundreds of moving pieces to make this work. Quality execution is needed to produce a new location, service, venue or church plant.

In many ways it is the effort of trying to plant a new church or campus every few months. For anyone who has planted something, you know what kinds of efforts that requires. This model requires consistent drive and management competence to execute on an ongoing basis all year long.

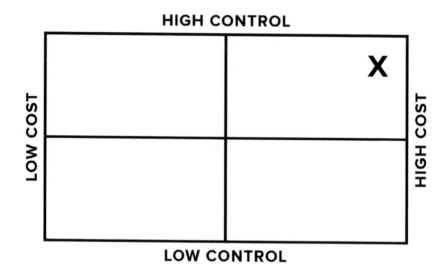

EXAMPLE CHURCHES

- Radiant Church - Pastor Aaron Burke - https://weareradiant.com

NEXT STEPS: What should I do if this is the model that I want to pursue?

1. Study the next Big Sunday hosted by Radiant Church and perhaps consider attending in-person.
2. Consider auditing the 'large launch' training that is taught in the CMN Launch Training.
3. Host your own Big Sunday Event and evaluate the results.
4. Start to plan how to use future Big Sunday Events to multiply a service, venue, location, or new church plant.

MODEL #10:
THE CELL-BASED MODEL

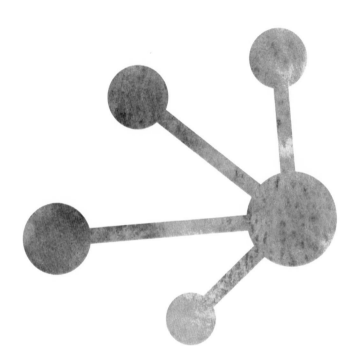

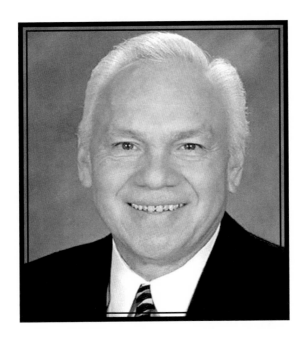

In 1926, in the midst of an explosion of Mexican immigration to Orange County, California, Templo Calvario was launched. Pastor Francisco Nieblas and his congregation began meeting in a small building in Santa Ana, California.

In the fall of 1976, the church had undergone a series of changes and had declined from 210 attendees to approximately 60. The pastor had been asked to leave, and the church was still reeling from the impact of this difficult season. During the search for a new leader, Daniel de Leon was asked to become the pastor, but he had some reservations: some of his family had been founding members of this church, and he had many family members who were still heavily involved at the church. Plus, he had more of a passion for youth ministry, but God confirmed to him that Templo Calvario was his next step. He accepted the role of Senior Pastor

In his first Sunday sermon as pastor, de León challenged the small congregation with this charge: "You are the evangelists." De León then began to introduce his congregation to the "Uno por Uno" (One by One) evangelism strategy and the ETC concept (Evangelize, Train & Commission). This was his God-given plan for church growth and member participation.

De Leon's methods took root, and it wasn't long before they needed a larger facility. On Thanksgiving Day 1977, Templo Calvario inaugurated their new sanctuary, holding five services each Sunday, three in Spanish and two in English. In this new location, the church quickly grew to more than 1,200.

THE ACCIDENTAL DISCOVERY

It was in the early 1980s that Templo Calvario began to discover its reproductive DNA. In 1982, a woman from Mexico gave her life to Christ at one of the services. For a period of time, she attended the church, got involved in a cell group, and was discipled. Then she simply disappeared.

Two years later, this same woman sent de León a letter informing him that she had moved back to Mexico and had started a church in her own backyard. The church had grown, and needed to rent a facility. De León began to encourage her and include her as a part of their larger vision.

Sometime later two members, also from Mexico, who had come to Christ at Templo, also felt called to go back to their hometowns and plant a new church. "Why do you want to do that? What is motivating you?," asked Daniel. They replied, "You told us 'We are the evangelists,' and when we heard you preach about planting new churches, we felt God was calling us to do that, too."

By the late 1980s de León and Templo Calvario had helped to open 18 churches in Mexico. Soon, these new pastors were asking, "Would you come and officially recognize these churches and tell us what to do?" De León worked with a Presbyter of the AG in Mexico, who allowed these new church plants to be overseen by de León, even though he was in a completely different nation.

To date, Templo Calvario has planted more than 100 new churches in both the USA and in Latin America, with about half in the USA and half in Latin America (primarily in Mexico). This movement is continuing to grow, and is currently "pregnant" with 20 pastors who are in the process of being trained and sent out as church planters..

Evangelize - Train - Commission
Templo Calvario follows this three step process:

1. Evangelize: Templo Calvario believes that every member of the Body of Christ has the responsibility to be an evangelist. "One for One" is the concept that those who attend church should bring someone with them. Christ won me so that I could win others. (Mark 1: 38-39)

2. Train: "Champions of Faith" is the church's training process. In whatever capacity you serve in the body of Christ, the word tells each believer to be prepared. (2 Timothy 4: 2)

3. Commission: After completing the "Champions of Faith" courses, the graduate is ready to be commissioned to launch a cell group in their own community to fulfill the vision Jesus gave in John 4:35, where He commissioned His followers to take the gospel to all nations, beginning at Jerusalem. Jerusalem is the local community!

SEVEN STEPS TO CELL-BASED REPRODUCTION

De León described what cell-based reproduction looks like. "We don't take dying churches and restart on those locations," he said. "We start brand new churches to reach brand new neighborhoods and communities."

STEP 1 - TRAIN

Once a leader is identified as a potential church planter, Templo Calvario gets them into an intensive discipleship process. The leaders begin by attending a three-night seminar and then attend a once-a-month training for a full year.

CEPI - Comisión Estratégica de Plantación de Iglesias (Strategic Commission for Church Planting) is the curriculum they use to train their leaders, which is also used throughout Latin America. Through this study they are:

- Doing demographic studies
- Learning about themselves and their personalities as leaders
- Defining their values and their DNA
- Receiving training from de León about what it takes to lead well, win souls, and multiply groups.

STEP 2 - START A CELL GROUP

Through starting a cell group, potential church leaders have the opportunity to prove their leadership skills. They can demonstrate that they can win people to Jesus and grow their group, that people want to follow them, and that they are able to effectively pastor their group members.

STEP 3 - MULTIPLY

Once they show that they can lead, they should begin to multiply. They should demonstrate that they can raise up a leader and help get another group started. After multiplying three times and having a cluster of cells, then they are ready to move to the next stage.

STEP 4 - THE RALLY

On occasion, we have the leader hold a "cell-abration" where every cell group in the cluster is encouraged to come together for a larger event. The purpose of this event is primarily evangelism. The focus is for every cell member to bring a friend that they are working to win to Christ. Once these monthly rallies are shown to be effective, church leaders legitimize this as a potential location for a new church.

STEP 5 - RENT A LOCATION - ESTABLISH A PREACHING POINT

These rallies then move into a monthly format. The leader begins to preach once a month to his or her cell clusters, as they gather. Templo Calvario pays for the expenses, and this new preaching-point begins to demonstrate its ability to grow and be viable. It is now that they start a kids ministry, along with many of the other functions of a local church.

STEP 6 - WEEKLY SERVICES - 'MISSION' STATUS

After six months to a year of effective monthly services, this new work is officially moved into the status of being a 'mission.' They begin to meet on Sunday mornings. The people who attend their cell-clusters, stop attending the parent church (Templo Calvario) and start attending their 'mission' location. A governance committee is established to work with and guide this new pastor, as the finances of the church are now being raised from within this new work as well as partially being supported by the Parent Church.

STEP 7 - ESTABLISHED AS A CHURCH

After three years of function as a mission, the church becomes official. They learn how to be self-supported. Templo limits its financial support, at this point, to $1,000 a month. Most often, the pastor now receives some type of part-time pay, but also works in some other job as well. "We don't want our churches or pastors to be saddled with any debt or financial pressure," described de León. "So we do not allow our churches to begin with matching funds of any kind."

If a church grows to some size, it then has the freedom to support its pastor full-time, and consider moving from PAC status to becoming a General Council church. "Not all of our church planters want to become General Council. Some choose to stay in the PAC format. We let the pastors decide," said de León.

```
┌─────────────────────────────────┐
│                                 │
│                                 │
│         C O R E   I D E A       │
│                                 │
│                                 │
└─────────────────────────────────┘
```

The Cell-Based Model operates by the principle that church planters are discovered within the church, and must be raised up through a process of action-oriented leadership which is proven through various stages of gathering people and reproducing disciples. This all happens in and through the cell groups and as they plant new churches

1. **What does each entity/location have in common?**

   Each location operates based on the same discipleship system. Everything begins and ends with the cell group. New believers are discipled, become apprentices, serve as Cell Group Leaders, multiply groups and leaders, then eventually have the opportunity to become a location and/or a new church.

2. **What is customized?**

   While the Cell-Based Model is designed to work in every community, each cell group leader determines where they meet and who they reach.

3. **What is centralized?**

   The training, system, and process are all designed centrally and executed locally. Each group is unique in the way they express themselves, but all follow the same plan and teaching material.

4. **What are the pros of this model?**

   This model provides a clear pathway for every person in the church to carry the vision and for young leaders to see the future pathway to become a leader within this movement. It is extremely cost effective, because there is little cost involved in starting cell groups. This model only invests financially in leaders once they have proven to be able to gather, disciple, and multiply.

5. What are the cons or limitations of this model?

The process for multiplication can at times feel slow and small. Investment in leaders from the ground up carries with it a lot of potential for failure and fall out. At the same time, there is a power and beauty about raising up leaders from within.

The system is built to sustain itself and grow. It is a methodologically 'pure' system, however, and **has to function with almost singular commitment to it**. Adding extra programming to a model like this not only clutters the process, but weighs down the multiplication potential.

6. What are the start-up and ongoing cost factors?

This may be the most cost-effective model. No real financial investments are made in a new work until there is enough momentum of multiplication to have an emerging congregation that helps to support its own public launch.

7. What is the level of management competence needed to provide proper controls?

While here is a need for management competence, it differs from what is needed in a multi-campus church. Since leaders are being raised up from within, the leaders who perform well and reproduce, are then able to manage and oversee the leaders they have raised up.

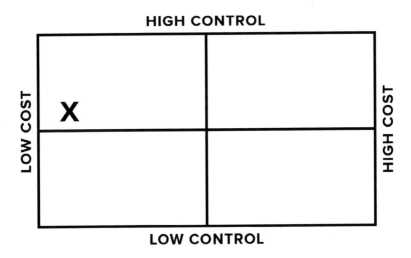

EXAMPLE CHURCHES

- Templo Calvario - Pastor Daniel de León - http://templocalvarioenglish.com/

NEXT STEPS: What should I do if this is the model that I want to pursue?

1. Research the CEPI Training - https://www.cepiad.com/
2. Visit a cell-based church and at least one of their cell groups.
3. If you already have small groups in your church, consider making some adjustments to your approach to fit with this style of multiplication.
4. Start to map out the region that your small groups currently meet.
5. Create a list of small group leaders with potential to become a church planter.
6. Start to cast vision for this pathway for future church planters.

MODEL #11:
THE PRISON CAMPUS MODEL

It seems that many of the growing churches have a
Lead Pastor who has the gift of evangelism. Pastor Herbert Cooper
of People's Church, based out of Oklahoma City, has just such

gifting and experience. People's Church has become a multi-racial, multi-generational, multi-campus church with nearly 6,000 people in attendance every weekend.

People's Church launched in an AMC Theater in 2002, in Oklahoma City. "That first summer was very difficult for us," shared Cooper. "I was used to traveling as an evangelist and speaking to large crowds. Now, I was preaching to a group of only 40 people. There were days we wondered if we had missed God!"

But in August, 2002, there was a turning point where they broke the 100 barrier. "We were ready to go crazy. I moonwalked. We danced. I think we might have even had a 'Jericho March' that day." By the fall they were pushing 200, and they continued to grow rapidly.

In 2006, the church moved into its first building, which triggered a new phase of rapid growth and bumped attendance to more than 1,000 every weekend. The second building, completed in 2010, launched People's Church into the megachurch category with more than 2,000 people attending weekly.

Shortly after that, Herbert and Tiffany started to dream about starting additional campuses. "Prior to 2010, we were always looking for ways to help church planters. We would raise money for them and provide coaching to some. We continue to do to this day," explained Cooper.

In 2012, People's Church took the step of starting its second location, in Midwest City, which was a twenty-minute drive from the original campus. They sent their worship pastor who had been raised in the church. He built a strong launch team and started the video-teaching campus in an old renovated movie theatre, leveraging Herbert's strong communication gifts. Within a few months, the Midwest Campus was averaging more than 1,000 people every weekend.

A few years later, in 2015, a third location was launched in the Northwest part of Oklahoma City. The Campus Pastors are a spiritual son and daughter to the Coopers, and have served with them for more than a decade. Today, the Northwest Campus is averaging more than 700 people every weekend.

THE VISION FOR A PRISON CAMPUS

Everything about the People's Church's approach to ministry sounds similar to the ATTRACTIONAL VIDEO VENUE MODEL as described in the first chapter of this book. People's Church is birthing branded campuses, with video teaching, and a centrally driven evangelistic emphasis. It is this very model which is naturally suited to take ministry and multiplication into one of the more unexpected and yet very needed places in our world...the prison system!

One of the video-venue locations of People's Church is a true expression of the heart of this church. "We started to ask the question, 'how do we make a difference in the lives of the' least of these'? How can we do that in Oklahoma,'" Cooper explained. "I am good friends with Jud Wilhite (Central Church, Las Vegas), and I watched as his church launched a video venue campus inside of a penitentiary. I watched what a difference it was making in the lives of these inmates."

People's Church cooperated with a ministry called God Behind Bars (Godbehindbars.com) to launch a campus in the Mabel Bassett Correctional Facility. It is the first 'prison church' in the state of Oklahoma, with more than 1,000 inmates in the system and is one of the largest women's prisons in the entire nation. Every weekend, there are now 200 women who gather as a part of this unique People's Church campus!

"I have a huge heart for this ministry! I have a family history that has been impacted by incarceration and all that that does to a family unit, so I am all in to see these women included into our fellowship," said Cooper. "Once or twice a year, I meet someone who has recently been released from prison and they start to attend one of our physical locations in person. What an amazing moment that is to hear them tell about how the prison campus changed their lives. Many have been water baptized, joined a small group, and started even to tithe!"

A CHURCH FOR EVERYBODY

The pain of Cooper's family experience birthed, both in him and in his church, a passion for people who are coming from broken, damaged, and difficult places. The motto for People's Church is, 'We are a church for EVERYBODY! A place where it's okay not to be okay! You can come as you are. But you won't stay as you are! Because you will encounter Jesus!'

This passion to reach everybody has resulted in a rhythmic strategic plan for outreach into the community. "We do a lot of outreach. It's a big part of who we are," said Cooper. We host a big Easter outreach every year, with carnival rides right on the property. We have huge prizes and giveaways. "

In the fall, People's Church hosts a Wild World Outreach as a back-to-school event with pony rides, face painting, snow cones and more. They also work with the Convoy of Hope to host a Day of Hope with free backpacks, haircuts, job fairs, and other practical ways to serve the community. "The goal at each one of these events is to preach the gospel and bring people to Christ."

Herbert and Tiffany have also established a vision for everybody, meaning people from various economic backgrounds, racial backgrounds, and generations. They are a powerful interracial couple, that teach and lead together. People's Church reflects this same value and dynamic in that it is approximately 65% black and 35% white. The staff reflects that same integrated reality.

"What we have built in our culture is beautiful, but it is also unique. Often those who are white, who attend People's Church are functioning under a black leader for the first time in their lives," explained Cooper. "And those who are black are attending church with non-blacks for the first time in their lives. It's both wonderful and amazing to see people take this journey with us."

Today, People's Church has an overall in-person attendance of more than 6,000 people every weekend, as well as an Online Campus

VISION FOR THE FUTURE

"Our goal is to continue to multiply by planting new churches and new campuses," explained Cooper. We currently have several staff members who feel called to plant a church. Our plan is to send them out and bless them to do what is in their heart to do." There are plans for church plants in Indianapolis, Des Moines, Tulsa, and Norman, Oklahoma.

"We also want to start more campuses. We feel that our best days are yet ahead, and we are in the process of reforming and building a better structure so that we can become even more effective at what we do," declared Cooper.

```
┌─────────────────────────────────┐
│                                 │
│                                 │
│          C O R E   I D E A      │
│                                 │
│                                 │
└─────────────────────────────────┘
```

The Prison Campus Model operates by the principle that a fully functioning church can be birthed behind the walls of a prison. Churches that function based on the Video Venue Teaching model are actually primed and ready to birth a prison campus. A prison campus is not just a once a week visit or a bible study but an actual campus of the overall church, where inmates become members, serve, and give, even prior to their release. After their release, they have church family on the outside that is waiting for them.

1. **What does each entity/location have in common?**

   The prison campus has the worship and message provided by livestream or recording. Volunteers staff the campus (both from within and from outside). The goal is for the prison campus to have as much in common with the other campuses as possible.

2. **What is customized?**

   The ministry is customized to fit the environment. Obviously, there are some limitations. but inmates serve on the welcome team, production team, prayer teams, and in other areas of ministry.

3. **What is centralized?**

   All programming and training is provided by a team sent from the parent church to lead the service and execute the plan on a weekly basis.

4. **What are the pros of this model?**

Inmates get to belong to a church while they serve time. The church family gets to know them and their families, and can provide discipleship, training, support, and ministry in a very personalized way.

5. What are the cons or limitations of this model?

There is very little downside to this plan. It does take a committed team of volunteers who are willing to carry the ministry on a regular basis. Ministry to those with a past can be fraught with disappointment and pain when some choose to go back to old ways. But the redemptive capacity of the church makes the effort worth it all.

6. What are the start-up and ongoing cost factors?

There is a significant initial cost investment involved in purchasing and installing the necessary equipment to broadcast the services within the prison campus. The ongoing costs are primarily focused around ministry to the families and to provide a pathway forward for those who exit the system.

7. What is the level of management competence needed to provide proper controls?

The management competence needed to launch a prison campus is not extremely high, if you are already functioning as a video venue church. It does require a leader who can oversee recruiting, training, mobilizing and organizing the volunteer teams who host the services.

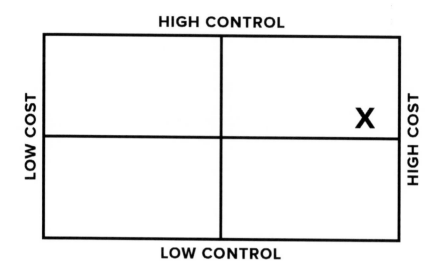

EXAMPLE CHURCHES

- Peoples Church - Herbert Cooper - peoples. church
- City First Church - Jeremy Deweert - cityfirst. church
- Red Rocks Church - redrocks.church
- Additional Resource: Godbehindbars.com

NEXT STEPS: What should I do if this is the model that I want to pursue?

1. Research State Prisons to find a location near you.
2. Connect with Godbehindbars.com.
3. Evaluate the startup cost and your church's readiness to produce an effective video-venue product.
4. Find leaders with a burden for this ministry
5. Send a team to see a Prison Campus in operation.

MODEL #12:
THE LEADERSHIP PIPELINE MODEL

Journey Church's mission statement is 'Love God more, and love more people!' To which they often add, 'The journey is always a step toward loving God more and loving more people.'

After Journey Church opened, it grew to 350 people in the first year. Pastor Jim Wilkes used his business training to plan for growth as a church. "In the first few years, church plants are just trying to survive. They are working out theories and strategies by trial and error," said Wilkes. "I remember being at McDonald's, ordering a McMuffin. I saw a sign that said, 'Six steps to a six figure income.' and thought 'if McDonald's has that kind of a plan for its franchise owners, we should have that kind of a plan for the church.'"

"The McDonald's plan is to move someone from burger flipper to six figure income. What if we had that kind of vision for every new believer who enters our church?"

This led to the development of an Ephesians 4 strategy to equip and disciple people into ministry. Wilkes began to outline steps that would take 'Joe Christ Follower' from being an unbeliever to a full-potential leader. Journey Church is wired to fulfill two values (love God and love people) and to help fulfill these values through volunteer leaders raised up through their leadership pipeline.

ONE CHURCH - MANY LOCATIONS - LED BY VOLUNTEERS

Journey Church is now one church in five locations, and they will soon be adding a sixth. In the early years, Journey Church's locations were run by paid Campus Pastors at each site. Today, they are transitioning to a model of volunteer-led campuses. "We have embraced an apostolic model that equips and mobilizes volunteers to be active in every aspect of leadership. We use volunteers to preach, lead worship, and manage ministry," said Wilkes.

Journey Church has a plan based on five levels of leadership:

1. Servant Leader
2. Next Level Leader
3. Team Leader
4. Coach

5. Director (Champion – which is a full-time staff member)

The first four levels are volunteers. Those who are paid, function as a Director who oversees several campuses and/or ministry departments. Seventy-five percent of all ministry at Journey Church is developed and led by volunteers.

This entire model was somewhat birthed out of need and frustration. "We would hire a Campus Pastor, but struggle to get them to function on their own. Often we felt the need to add an administrator to work with them, which increased the cost of starting and managing a campus," described Wilkes. Eventually, they realized that some of their volunteers were already outperforming some of the paid staff. But these volunteers were unwilling, due to career and finances, to leave their jobs.

The decision was made to build the model on **high-capacity volunteer leadership.**

"Actually, God used the frustration we experienced to change our heart," declared Wilkes. "I believe that the next reformation is going to be an Ephesians 4 movement that emphasizes the 'priesthood of all believers.' Ephesians 4 states that when people engage in ministry, the church becomes more mature and starts to move into the fullness of Christ. This is what Journey Church is starting to see happen."

Journey Church now has a hybrid of paid and volunteer staff who preach on the weekends. There is a dual approach to communication. At times, there is a broadcasted message by video. "We can broadcast to any campus, from any campus," explained Wilkes. "But we also have a teaching team of four-to-five communicators (some paid and some volunteer)in a speaking rotation.

Some weeks, the message from a teaching team member is broadcast to all locations, while other weeks, all six campuses have live preaching, using the same message.

Communicators are not necessarily campus overseers or ministry directors. The goal is to focus on the function and the spiritual gift, rather the role and whether the communicator is paid or a volunteer. "We lean into our function, but we release the gift to where it benefits the organization most," explained Wilkes.

THE VISION

The current vision of Journey Church is to have 12 campuses within the next five years, all across the Greater Cleveland area. Each campus will be at least 15 minutes from one another in a different quadrant of the region. "If we are able to accomplish this, Journey Church will be within a reasonable driving distance for the 1.9 million people in the area that have no current church affiliation," said Wilkes. "God gave me the promise that if we would do this, we would see the spiritual climate of the region change by loving and serving our community, while remaining connected together!"

Currently, with six locations, Journey Church is reaching about 2,700 people every weekend. But the vision is not exclusively to plant campuses. Journey Church has also chosen to help plant self-governing churches that are not part of the Journey Campus family. They do this through giving to ARC (Association of Related Churches), to the Ohio Church Multiplication Network and by actively being involved in coaching pastors, planters, and leaders.

Wlikes is now trying to dedicate 50% of his time to coach pastors and leaders on church health. His recent bout with cancer brought additional clarity to his life. "Having cancer was a wakeup call," said Wilkes. "In a way it was one of the best things that could happen because it freed me from some of the things I was striving to accomplish, that are honestly not that important. During my struggle with cancer, all I thought about was my wife and my kids. I didn't think at all about the church."

"I had previously worried so much about the church," said Wilkes. "But when I was diagnosed with cancer, I learned what I really valued. Jesus spoke to me 'Jim I never asked you to die for my church, I want you to serve her. Lay your life down for your wife and your family.'"

Wilke's vision now has also expanded to teach pastors and leaders that it is possible to have a growing church and a healthy life and family. "Too many pastors are not living healthy lives, "noted Wilkes. This awareness has translated into a strategy on how to invest his time and resources. "I don't just do ministry, I now do ministry through people, to people." declared Wilkes. "God began to unfold a picture to me of a car dealership. 'Your showroom is great. You can display the cars. But your factory is too small. You need to build your leadership factory to 10 times the size to produce the vehicle you need to reach the community.'"

"When you produce leaders, leaders attract leaders, and it keeps rolling," said Wilkes. "Today Journey Church looks like everything I thought it was going to look like, and everything I never knew it would look like. Watching Jesus build His church has been astounding to me."

```
┌─────────────────────────────────────┐
│                                     │
│                                     │
│          C O R E   I D E A          │
│                                     │
│                                     │
└─────────────────────────────────────┘
```

The Leadership Pipeline Model operates by the principle that new campuses and new ministries provide an opportunity to develop new leaders on every level. This model prioritizes the development of the leader over the development, growth, size, or quality of the location. This model is willing to accept slower progress in growth to gain greater momentum in leadership development.

1. What does each entity/location have in common?

Each location shares the commitment to leadership development, and the process of mentoring relationships needed to raise up the next wave of leaders. Every church that functions using this model makes decisions on a continuum as to what aspect of the church will be common and which will be customized. Most often, as in the case of Journey Church, all locations carry the same brand but may be customized based on the demographics of the community and of the personality of the local leadership.

2. What is customized?

Each campus has a live speaker, so as to develop skilled communicators. The messages are often prepared in community but delivered in the unique voice and style of the individual communicator. This same approach is taken with their worship leaders as well.

Much of the overall church brand and DNA is maintained at each location in the areas of programming, events, language, and approach. But there is some freedom of expression given to the developing leaders in the pipeline.

3. What is centralized?

Much of what is centralized in an Attractional Video Venue Model is also centralized in a Leadership Pipeline Model: one set of books, one board that governs all the locations, one communication department, a sermon development team, a social media department, and a programming team. Every team member, at the locations, receives training and coaching from those on the staff that are experts in their field.

4. What are the pros of this model?

The goal of this model is developing and equipping leaders through active learning, mentoring, feedback, encouragement, and opportunities to fail or succeed. Leaders in these environments are proven before they are put into positions, but they also learn while on the job. The primary benefit of this model is the opportunity to develop many leaders, who live in community, share common values, and celebrate one another's success.

There is also the value of developing local leaders, through apprenticeship. There are several churches mentioned below in the 'example churches' section that have committed to having apprentices in place at every key position, and at every location. Both Pastors Nate Ruch and Wes Davis see multiple locations and a methodology that requires multiplication of leaders. Every campus and every position is an opportunity for every leader to reproduce.

5. What are the cons or limitations of this model?

Sometimes, the levels of excellence and quality can suffer while a leader is learning a new skill, which has the potential of slowing growth at their location.

6. What are the start-up and ongoing cost factors?

When a new location begins, the investment in facilities, equipment, marketing and staff are the same as any other multi-campus launch.

The goal of the model is to launch large enough so the new campus is healthy and can continue to grow and cover ongoing costs. The risk is that if growth slows, the campus may struggle to pay the bills and may need help from the parent organization to remain open and functioning.

7. What is the level of management competence needed to provide proper controls?

There is a high degree of management competence needed in a Leadership Development Model. While the main goal in this model may not be to manage excellence of execution as much as it is to manage the people development processes, the decentralized multi-level management of people can be complicated and complex and requires a leader and a team that is committed to this model.

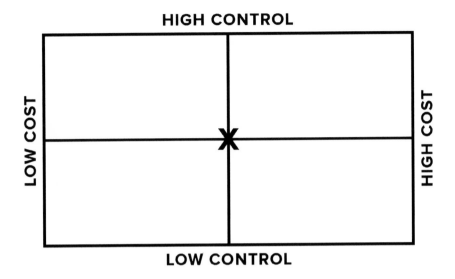

HIGH CONTROL

LOW COST

HIGH COST

LOW CONTROL

EXAMPLE CHURCHES

- New Life Church - Wes Davis - newlife.tv
- Journey Church - Jim Wilkes - journey.church
- Emmaneul Church - Nate Ruch - emmanuelcc.org

NEXT STEPS: What should I do if this is the model that I want to pursue?

1. Pray over your region and consider where there might most be a need for a new venue, new campus, or new church.

2. Consider how multiplying a new venue, new church, or new campus might provide you with a greater opportunity to develop leaders.

3. Visit a Leadership Development Model church to see how their processes work.

4. Begin to evaluate your leadership pipeline. How does your church develop leaders?

5. Start to apply the 'apprenticeship' principle where every key leader selects and intentionally develops another leader in their role.

6. Experiment with multiplying an additional service and raising up the leaders needed to effectively duplicate what you were doing in your other services or events.

EPILOGUE:
THE EXPERIMENTAL MODEL
OF MULTIPLICATION

Before I conclude this book, I want to offer one final story of multiplication from Pastor Mark and Lora Batterson, who founded and continue to lead National Community Church in the heart of Washington, DC. Mark is famous for a statement regarding one of his church's key values, which is a foundational principle for innovation in his ministry.

"Everything is an experiment!"
I find this statement to be true, especially in the arena of church multiplication. No one begins the journey toward multiplication with everything figured out. Similarly, no one begins the journey as a new parent with everything figured out! You have to give birth to something before you discover how you are going to manage your growing family.

**MARK BATTERSON
NATIONAL COMMUNITY
CHURCH(NCC)**

NCC is one church in seven locations, in some of the most highly trafficked areas of our nation's capital. National Community Church has met in the theaters at Union Station, in the coffeehouse chain they founded called Ebenezers, in a DC Dream Center location, and now in the Lincoln Theater.

While Batterson might be most easily recognized as a prolific author, with many of his books like *Circle Maker*, *Whisper*, *Graver Robber*, and *Play the Man* making the *New York Times* Best Sellers lists, he has also been an innovator and leader in church multiplication. In one of his early books, *In a Pit with a Lion*, Mark describes the first few steps he took to plant a church:

"When I was in graduate school in the Chicago area, Lora and I wanted to plant a church on Chicago's North Shore. We had a core group. We had a name. We set up a bank account. One minor detail: We never had a service.

That failed attempt was acutely embarrassing because we told everybody that we were going to plant a church, and then we fell flat on our faces. And it was disillusioning because we thought that's what God wanted us to do. It was a complete failure. But it was also one of the best things that ever happened to us. It's not that I like failing any more now than I did then, but somehow that experience released us from the fear of failure. It built up fear immunity. So when we had the opportunity to become part of planting National Community Church, we weren't afraid to fail. I figured we couldn't do any more damage than we had done in Chicago!"[7]

I intentionally placed Batterson's story at the end of this book, because his approach is something that every successful multiplying church and pastor has at their core. They are willing to step out and try some things. They take risks. They attempt approaches to ministry that are unproven and may be very unique. They are willing to fail. Listen to Mark's words on this matter:

**"*Most of us want absolute certainty before we step out in faith. We love 100-percent money-back guarantees. But the problem with that is this: It takes faith out of the equation. There's no such thing as risk-free faith. And you can't experience success without risking failure."[8]*

In every chapter of this book, I have attempted to capture the different approaches to multiplication by defining what they 'model'. Batterson models 'experimental multiplication.' When I asked Mark to describe the NCC story of multiplication, he replied, "To be honest, it's been a bit all over the place. I mean I know we have done some things well, and other things not so much. It's been a process of discovery."

To which I responded, "Actually, I wouldn't describe your model as being all over the place, it's that you have consistently and regularly experimented with new ways of doing church. You have held church services in locations and in ways that are truly unique. You are living out what you have indicated is a value- 'Everything is an experiment!'"

Again, listen to Mark tell the story of how NCC began:

"In 1996, I inherited a small core group of people and began serving as lead pastor at National Community Church. We got off to a rather inauspicious start. Our first Sunday was the weekend the blizzard of ' 96 dumped record snowfalls on Washington, DC . Only three people made it to church our first Sunday – my wife, my son Parker, and myself.

"Of course, the upside is that we experienced a 633 percent growth spurt our second Sunday when nineteen people showed up.

"For the first nine months, our average attendance was 25 people. And that included the Father, Son, and Holy Spirit on a good Sunday. I used to close my eyes in worship because it was too depressing to keep them open. I hate to even admit this, but I honestly don't think I would have attended the church if I hadn't been the pastor. According to church demographers, more than half of all church plants never see their second year. And when I look in the rearview mirror, I can see how NCC could have easily padded that statistic.

"During those first few months, I didn't really feel like a pastor, and NCC didn't really feel like a church. It felt like we were thrown into the deep end and none of us knew how to swim. We were just thrashing around trying to keep our heads above water. Then in September of 1996 we experienced what I perceived as a huge problem. The person in charge of leasing public schools left a voicemail informing us that the DC public school we had been meeting in was being closed because of fire code violations.

"I wish I could say that my initial reaction was one of faith. But the truth is, I had this sickening feeling in the pit of my stomach. We didn't even feel like a church yet, and we were on the verge of becoming a homeless church. I wrote these words in my journal on September 27, 1996 :'I feel like we've been backed into a corner.' It honestly seemed as if we had fallen into a pit with a lion on a snowy day. But what I saw as a daunting problem turned out to be a five-hundred-pound opportunity. We started exploring rental options on Capitol Hill, and only one door opened: the movie theaters at Union Station.

"In retrospect, I can't imagine a more strategic location for a church plant. Union Station is the most visited destination in Washington, DC. More than 25 million people pass through the station every year. We have our own parking garage, subway system, and bus stop. There are 40 food-court restaurants right outside our theater marquee. And the station is strategically located four blocks from the Capitol and four blocks from the largest homeless shelter in the city.

God perfectly positioned us right in the middle of the marketplace, and we wouldn't want to be anywhere else. Doing church in the middle of the marketplace is part of our DNA. In fact, our long-term vision is to meet in movie theaters at metro stops throughout the DC area. But here's the thing: It took a setback to get us where God wanted us to go. It took a God-ordained opportunity that came as a really well-disguised problem."[9]

Now, it's important to remember that at this time, multi-site churches were in the formative stages, and in only a few locations around the country. Certainly, there was no multi-site manual for Batterson to follow. Second, very few, if any, churches were meeting in movie theaters. It was a concept that was untested and unproven. But soon a second campus, launched in 2003, gave birth to the experimental model of video teaching. What a great place to try it out! Movie theaters with an auditorium with a huge screen was a perfect spot to attempt such an experiment.

Batterson's vision for campuses in movie theatres along metro stops rapidly expanded, adding new campuses in 2005, 2007, 2008, and 2009.

Another key innovation happened during those early days of multiplication:

When National Community Church was getting off the ground, our church office was a spare bedroom in our house. Then our daughter, Summer, was born, and that room doubled as an office by day and bedroom by night. We would set up and tear down her portable crib every day, but that got real old real fast, so we started aggressively looking for office space for the church. Over the course of the next four months, we found two places that seemed to be perfect, and we put contracts on both of them—but both contracts fell through.

It honestly felt like God had pulled the carpet out from under our feet twice. Then I was walking home from Union Station one day, and I passed in front of a row house at 205 F Street, NE. There was no "For Sale" sign or "For Rent" sign, but I felt prompted to call the owner. Somehow the Holy Spirit surfaced his name out of the recesses of my subconscious. That is the only way I can describe it. I had met the owner a year before, but I'm not great with names. To be honest, I wasn't 100 percent sure the name that surfaced was really the owner's name, but I looked it up in the phone book and dialed the number.

I introduced myself, and before I could tell him why I was calling, he interrupted me and said, "I was just thinking about you. In fact, I was going to give you a call. I'm thinking about putting 205 F Street on the market, and I was wondering if you'd be interested." God's timing is impeccable! Not only did we purchase 205 F Street, but it gave us a foothold on the adjacent property at 201 F Street. I can't tell you how many times we laid hands on those brick walls at 205 F Street and asked God to give us the adjoining property. That adjoining property is now Ebenezers Coffeehouse."[10]

Ebenezers Coffeehouse not only became the location of the NCC offices, it also housed a campus that met on Saturday nights, as a small intimate venue. It was from Ebeneezers that Mark and his teaching team began filming their messages, which would then be broadcast on the big screens in every movie theater in their campus family.

In addition, the coffee house became a significant funding stream for ministry. "Ebenezers Coffeehouse has served more than a million customers and given more than one million dollars from its net profits to kingdom causes."[11] (Batterson, Mark. In a Pit with a Lion on a Snowy Day (p. 10). The Crown Publishing Group. Kindle Edition.)

Innovation was birthed out of need. "We were multi-site out of necessity. It was the only way we could grow in the urban context. It was affordable for us. But it also was the way that the Lord chose to grow us," explains Batterson.

For the first 23 years of NCC's history, they did not own any church buildings. Over the years, their locations have been creative and unique, and all of them right in the middle of the marketplace.

- Movie Theaters

- Coffeehouse
- Warehouses
- Performance Theater
- Night Club

Currently an 1891 Navy Yard Car Barn, a historic location where street cars were able to turn around and span a city block, is being renovated to house a functional movie theater, a co-op working space, a restaurant, a coffeehouse, child development center, and another NCC campus.

The intentionality to meet in spaces in the marketplace has a theology of reaching a city, based on Jeremiah, in chapter 29:

This what the LORD Almighty, the God of Israel, says to all those I carried into exile from Jerusalem to Babylon: "Build houses and settle down; plant gardens and eat what they produce. Marry and have sons and daughters; find wives for your sons and give your daughters in marriage, so that they too may have sons and daughters. Increase in number there; do not decrease. **Also, seek the peace and prosperity of the city to which I have carried you into exile. Pray to the LORD for it, because if it prospers, you too will prosper."**

For I know the plans I have for you," declares the LORD, "plans to prosper you and not to harm you, plans to give you hope and a future. Then you will call on me and come and pray to me, and I will listen to you.[11]

"Our goal is not just to create a space to have church services, but rather to bless our city in everything that we do as a church," said Batterson. "We are always experimenting, not just with new ways to plant, but with new ways to serve and lift the people who live in our city. When Jeremiah gave this challenge, it was not a short-term vision, but a 70-year plan. We are now working from a strategy to bless our city over a series of generations."

LEVERAGING RESOURCES FOR CHURCH PLANTING

The next thing on the horizon for NCC? 'We want to leverage what we have learned in DC, by backing, sending, and resourcing church planters in other cities." Currently there are plans to plant in Chicago, Nashville, and Baltimore. NCC has also had a large initiative to plant internationally in Ethiopia as well.

To prepare for more planters, NCC has a 'church planter in residence' program where a potential planter joins the team at NCC for one year. The goal is that they download the DNA of the house, breath in the air, and learn the skills of pastoring directly from one of the NCC Campus Pastors. They also get a glimpse of the roles and responsibilities of key department leaders as they spend time with the team.

NCC has also decided to give something financially to bless every church plant in Washington, DC, regardless of denomination. "We do that to keep our heart in the right place and to be a shareholder in whatever God is doing in our city."

CONCLUDING THOUGHTS

What we can learn from Pastor Mark Batterson, and from every one of the pastors and churches that we have studied in this book, is that multiplication is a process of discovery. It involves wanting to serve the purpose of God creatively. It's a reflection of a passion to serve a community, city, region, or unreached people. It's never perfect. It's never easy.

But it is so worth every step of attempted obedience! I pray that God would grant you favor, discernment, and courage as you take the next steps on your own personal journey.

NOTES

1 Matthew 6:33

2 Rob Ketterling, Fix It. Whose Problem Is It? (United States: River Valley Resources, 2008), 13-16.

3 Ketterling, Fix It. Whose Problem Is It?, 13-16.

4 AG Trust, "City Church Tulsa" AG Trust Assemblies of God, May 1, 2020, https://agtrust.org/en/articles/plant-churches/2020_may-4_city-church_tulsa_ok?D=4C5623E5040049B59B53412EE65C0117

5 Ginger Kobaba, "Every Zip Code for Christ," Assemblies of God, June 19, 2018, https://news.ag.org/es-ES/News/Every-Zip-Code-for-Christ

6 "Senior Pastors", New Birth Church, accessed February 20, 2021, http://newsite2.mynewbirth.church/newsite2/478-2/

7 Mark Batterson, In a Pit with a Lion on a Snowy Day: How to Survive and Thrive When Opportunity Roars, (United States: Multnomah, 2016), 54.

8 Batterson, In a Pit with a Lion on a Snowy Day: How to Survive and Thrive When Opportunity Roars, 118.

9 Batterson, In a Pit with a Lion on a Snowy Day: How to Survive and Thrive When Opportunity Roars, 63-64.

10 Batterson, In a Pit with a Lion on a Snowy Day: How to Survive and Thrive When Opportunity Roars, 140

11 Jeremiah 29:11